God Leads in Perplexities, Joys, and Sorrows

by
Iris Hayden Stober
with Carolyn Byers

TEACH Services, Inc.
PUBLISHING
www.TEACHServices.com • (800) 367-1844

World rights reserved. This book or any portion thereof may not be copied or reproduced in any form or manner whatever, except as provided by law, without the written permission of the publisher, except by a reviewer who may quote brief passages in a review.

This book was written to provide truthful information in regard to the subject matter covered. The author assumes full responsibility for the accuracy of all facts and quotations as cited in this book. The opinions expressed in this book are the author's personal views and interpretation of the Bible, Spirit of Prophecy, and/or contemporary authors and do not necessarily reflect those of TEACH Services, Inc.

This book is sold with the understanding that the publisher is not engaged in giving spiritual, legal, medical, or other professional advice. If authoritative advice is needed, the reader should seek the counsel of a competent professional.

Copyright © 2013 TEACH Services, Inc.
ISBN-13: 978-1-4796-0062-5 (Paperback)
ISBN-13: 978-1-4796-0063-2 (ePub)
ISBN-13: 978-1-4796-0064-9 (Kindle/Mobi)
Library of Congress Control Number: 2013931058

Published by

www.TEACHServices.com • (800) 367-1844

Dedication

This book is dedicated to Carmen, my joy and reason for living after the accident.

Acknowledgment

Iris became acquainted with Carolyn Byers in Sequim, Washington, where Carolyn's parents had retired. Iris and Al ministered to Carolyn's aging parents, particularly while the Byers were working in Togo. While in Togo, Iris' book (co-authored by Dr. Barry Wecker) *The Church Health Educator* was highly recommended to the Byers by Dr. George Sanz, then health director for West Africa.

After writing down her memories, Carolyn approached Iris and asked her if she could edit the manuscript and prepare it for publication. While she was working on the book, Carolyn was diagnosed with pancreatic cancer and passed away a few months later. During this time she became like a sister to Iris, and Iris acknowledges that without Carolyn this book would not be a reality.

Curiously, several places in this book are also familiar to the Byers: LeRoy spent a summer in Peru as a student missionary. The Byers family spent three months in Puerto Rico when LeRoy did a mission elective as part of his training at Loma Linda University. Also, Iris mentions her visit to Maluti Hospital in Lesotho, the Byers' home for twelve years where Dr. Byers served as the ophthalmologist.

Carolyn authored the *Forever Stories* set; *Lucy Miller, The Girl Who Waited for Jesus; Good Night Too Soon;* and *Mary Andrews, Companion of Sorrows*, plus various articles in the *Adventist Review* and children's magazines. With her ophthalmologist husband, Dr. LeRoy Byers, Carolyn spent twenty-three years in overseas mission service in Taiwan, Lesotho, and Togo. The Byers have four children: Brenda, Branton, Brady, and Brani.

Table of Contents

Introduction	....	7
Chapter 1	The Fifth Girl	9
Chapter 2	Farm-Grown	13
Chapter 3	The Heart of My Inspiration	17
Chapter 4	God Stands at the Fork in the Road	24
Chapter 5	In the Days of My Youth	29
Chapter 6	God's Footprints are in the Shadows	36
Chapter 7	Pastures Green; Waters Still	46
Chapter 8	In Righteous Paths, Puerto Rico	49
Chapter 9	New Righteous Paths, Nicaragua	54
Chapter 10	Yea, Though I Cry	62
Chapter 11	Supported by God's Staff	66
Chapter 12	Remembering Them	70
Chapter 13	Restoring My Soul	73
Chapter 14	Nicaraguan Graduation	78
Chapter 15	Nothing Lacking, Seattle	80

Chapter 16	My Cup Runs Over, Honduras	85
Chapter 17	In Unfamiliar Paths, The GC	92
Chapter 18	His Sheep Know His Voice, London	99
Chapter 19	Faithful Shepherd, First Promise Fulfilled	101
Chapter 20	Faithful Shepherd, Second Promise Fulfilled	105
Chapter 21	Faithful Shepherd, Third Promise Fulfilled	109
Chapter 22	His Goodness And Mercy	112
Chapter 23	In The House of My Lord	120
Epilogue		124

Introduction

It was a rainy Sabbath afternoon in Nicaragua, a Central American country sandwiched between Costa Rica and Honduras. From my front room window, I surveyed the campus of Hospital Adventista de Nicaragua. The hospital was nestled in a valley on the outskirts of a village called La Trinidad. In the dry season, the grass seemed to wear khaki, but on this day in 1970, they were dressed in a lively green. From my vantage point, I could see the hospital, school of nursing buildings, church, and staff homes.

My husband, Dick, served as a Bible teacher for the school of nursing, chaplain for the hospital, and pastor of the hospital church. He was also assigned to oversee all the churches in the northern part of Nicaragua and serve as youth director for the Nicaraguan Mission. Along with juggling my responsibilities as a pastor's wife and a mother of three, I was an instructor in the school of nursing. It did not take long to learn that living on a hospital campus meant becoming entangled in a myriad of other duties.

On a usual Sabbath afternoon, we ferried nursing students to nearby villages for branch Sabbath Schools. However, on this Sabbath, rain kept us home. Instead, several staff members migrated to our house for Sabbath dinner. After the meal, 11-year-old Richie, 7-year-old Carmen, and 5-year-old Rodney played quietly with their friends in the living room with the toys we had saved especially for Sabbaths. The adults lingered at the table.

The conversation turned to God's leading: How could one know how God wants us to prioritize our lives?

Recounting various Bible stories, someone mentioned that God had personally and directly instructed Abraham what to do, where to go, and when to do it. We observed that though many Bible characters had experienced direct guidance from God, none of us had. We looked at Gideon, who asked for the sign of the fleece. We noted that his method was unusual and speculated this should be used only in extreme cases. We remembered the Urim and Thummim, the two stones embedded in the breastplate of Israel's high priest. In those times men could ask God for guidance through the high priest; in response, God would answer with a "yes" or "no" using the Urim and Thummim stones. Again, that method of communicating with God was not available to us today. We concluded our happy interchange with the sentiment that God leads each of us in different ways, depending on our individual personalities and our distinctive walk with Him.

That conversation inspired me to search the subject for myself. I learned in the writings of Ellen White that God reveals His will to us in three ways: through His Word, through providential workings, and through the appeals of the Holy Spirit making impressions upon the heart (*Testimonies for the Church,* vol. 5, p. 512).

As I thought on this, I realized I was dealing with topics too vast to quickly understand, but I determined to learn more about how God guides His children and, specifically, to study God's leading in my life.

What I didn't know, and what no one seated at our dining room table on that rainy day knew, was that tragedy would shatter my family in a short five months. Not one person there had the slightest inkling that I would soon bury the husband sitting beside me and two of my children that were then quietly playing on the floor. I could not have realized that I would need that conversation to seed my thoughts and help me through that heart-crushing time and beyond.

Over my lifetime I have pondered and studied the theme of that conversation, and I still grapple for understanding and expect I will continue struggling until I reach heaven. However, through the years my conclusions have matured into a settled realization that God has dealt faithfully with me. Though I am a private person, though retelling this story opens old wounds, and though it generates new tears, I want to share my testimony. As you read, I hope you recognize that *Yea, Though I Cry,* God has been with me now some 70 years, and my God will be with you too.

Chapter 1

The Fifth Girl

In 1933, my parents, Howard and Minnie Hansen, lived on the Ayrshire farm near Ruthven, Iowa. Dad loved those rolling hillocks where his potatoes grew as big as bricks, and his corn produced ears nearly a foot long. Selling milk, eggs, chickens, and garden produce provided weekly spending money. A part of the oats, corn, and alfalfa was sold for cash at harvest time, while the remainder was kept to feed the livestock and stored in the big barn and out-lying sheds. Besides the outbuildings, there was a white, wooden two-story house with a spacious front porch which rollicked with the activity and laughter of four girls—Stella, MaryEtta, Rozella ("Rosy"), and Shirley. Soon a fifth child would bless the home.

In that Scandinavian community, and especially in our Danish and German family culture, sons were important. Dad, of course, wanted a boy to help tend the farm. Carl, Dad's older brother, had openly voted for a boy. Carl, himself, had four boys, so he thought he understood his brother's situation because he wanted a girl more than anything. Besides, surely the odds were that after four girls, my parents could expect a boy!

On December 4, 1933, Dad drove his tractor through the falling snow to use the neighbor's phone to call the doctor. Mom was in labor. Eventually, the doctor arrived along with the neighbor lady. Hospitals at that time were seen by many as a place to die, so most babies were delivered at home. Not long after their arrival, I made my entrance into the world, a healthy, blue-eyed, fair-skinned tow-head. But what a disappointment! Here was another daughter, the *fifth* girl.

Even though the family had hoped for a boy, Mom and my four sisters had considered the possibility that they might need another girl's name. When Mom was pregnant with me, she often read *The Bedtime Stories* to my sisters. The one the girls liked the most was, "Iris Does the Ironing." As the story goes, little Iris was left alone for a few minutes while her mother ran to the store. Her mother instructed Iris not to touch the iron. Though she was fine at first, Iris decided she wanted to "help" her mother by doing the ironing. This resulted in burning the ironing board and ruining her favorite dress, as well as her mother's best dress. So, my sisters wanted me to be named "Iris." As for a middle name, Mom chose "Sadie," which originated with my mother's older sister. All the girls in my family were given middle names honoring relatives, except MaryEtta. Her first name combined the names of two relatives. So, after much deliberation, I became "Iris," Iris Sadie Hansen.

When it came time for my oldest sister, Stella, to go to school, Dad and Mom talked long and hard over what they should do. It was two "country" miles to the rural school, a bit far for a first-grader to walk alone each day. It was neither convenient nor a good use of work time for Dad to leave his farm work each day to drive Stella to school. If Mom were to escort her, she would have to bundle up the younger ones and take them along. They decided that the best solution was for Stella to live with Grandma and Grandpa Hansen in Ruthven and attend school in town.

So, little Stella moved to Ruthven, but on weekends she returned home. This worked well except for one minor detail. Living in the country meant we had not been exposed to childhood communicable diseases, and, you guessed it, Stella contracted chicken pox. She didn't get very ill, but she managed to bring it home to all four of her younger siblings, who became miserably sick. Other diseases followed. Eventually, Stella brought home whooping cough, the well-known killer of children. My sisters recovered quickly, but I wasn't even a year old at the time, and I did not get well. After my high-pitched "whoops" subsided, the dreaded pneumonia took possession of me.

The doctor came but offered little hope for my recovery.

Mom asked him, "Shouldn't we take her to the hospital?"

"Mrs. Hansen," he responded, "You are taking as good care of her as they would in the hospital. Besides, either in the hospital or at home, it is improbable she will survive."

The doctor knew all too well what happened to many young children with this disease. If they didn't die of asphyxia or convulsions, brain damage might take them. Antibiotics, the wonder drugs of the future, were still being developed. In another six years, doctors could vaccinate children against pertussis (whooping cough), but nothing was able to help me.

This placed an overwhelming responsibility on my young mother. She and Dad prayed earnestly over me, "Please God, give us wisdom. Give Iris healing. We don't want to lose this child. We know many other people have lost their children to whooping cough, but, Lord, please heal this one!"

Church members and extended family learned of our crisis and also prayed. This baby girl who should have been a boy had become incredibly special to the family and surrounding community.

Mom's father, Daniel Johnson, had once worked at the Battle Creek Sanitarium in Michigan. It was there that he had learned about hydrotherapy. He had taught this method of healing to my Mom, and she now applied that knowledge to my care. She gave me hot and cold treatments, mustard plasters, cold compresses, steam, as well as other techniques she had learned. She moved my small crib to the dining room so she could monitor me while still caring for the family. For weeks, she treated me. It was no easy task to repeatedly boil up cotton pads, wring them out with towels and old sheets, wrap them in wool, and place them strategically on my soft baby skin so as not to burn me but still produce the best circulation possible.

There were times when my fingers and ears were so transparent that Mom thought I had died, but after a moment, I took another breath. No, God did not suddenly heal me, but he did give Mom wisdom in caring for me. At last, the infection subsided, but it was many months, perhaps years, before I looked like a healthy child.

That was a tough year for Mom and Dad. The depression, though partially over, continued to make life difficult. Money was in short supply. With all the children sick and the baby barely surviving with pneumonia, it was a long, long winter. There was little time to visit neighbors, and no one in my family was able to go to church. In addition, while Mom was struggling to keep up with the housework, another baby was on its way. Fortunately, Dad had learned how to do some cooking and could help her, though this made it difficult to keep up with the outside work. Occasionally, a teenage girl came out to help him.

In February, the new baby arrived: a son which they named Lyle. Finally, Howard and Minnie Hansen had their boy. This time Uncle Carl approved. That event was a joyous occasion and the high point of the year.

In the spring of 1934, after my pneumonia had cleared, Mom and Dad decided they should visit Minnesota to see Mom's relatives. Once we arrived, Grandma Johnson took one look at me and declared, "Minnie, I don't think that baby is going to make it."

Mom was devastated. After all the work and prayers she had invested in this child, she had to ask herself once again, "Am I going to lose Iris?"

Fortunately, Grandma Johnson's prediction never came true.

Many years later, my mom and I were looking at pictures, and I asked, "Why are there no baby pictures of me?"

She replied, "My child, you looked so

The six of us paused in our work of getting corn cobs for the stove. I am peaking around the door.

scrawny and so sickly that you would not have wanted any pictures."

Of course, I do not remember all this history. These stories were told to me many times by Dad and Mom. They always emphasized their belief that it was a miracle I healed from whooping cough and pneumonia. As I was growing up, they repeatedly said, "God saved you for a purpose."

This impacted my life in a grand way. Like every child on earth should feel, I felt special and that I was destined for some unique and important work.

Chapter 2

Farm-Grown

The country was a great place to raise children. Dad set up an old stove in the "grove," a thick line of trees he had planted as a windbreak. There my siblings and I "cooked and baked" mud pies and imaginary pastries. Sometimes we were even allowed to build a real fire in the stove and fry pancakes on it.

The farm animals seemed like pets. There was Chase, the cow, and Dad's beloved team of horses that would stop and go at his "giddy-up" and "whoa." Oh, and I mustn't forget Tippy, a small black dog with a white patch on the end of his tail. Tippy thought he owned our rocking chair and would stare off anyone who got there first. My favorite pets were the barn cats. In the fall I would bury them in piles of dry leaves just to see them burst out. They would let me dress them in the doll clothes I had made, and it was always fun to squirt milk into their mouths at milking time.

Dad had grown up on an Iowa farm where his Danish father had taught him the secrets of farming. Unfortunately, his father only sent him to school during the months when the farm work was light. Thus, Dad never learned to read well. However, when he was a child, his father did take him to church every Sabbath where he learned to love the Adventist message. Sadly, when Dad was a teenager, his family distanced themselves from the church over some disagreement. This forced Dad to choose for himself how he would relate to church. Dad decided to stand firm for his Lord, a commitment he maintained throughout his life. Of the eleven siblings, only Dad and one sister stayed in the Seventh-day Adventist church.

Eventually, Dad was determined to find an Adventist wife. This was a problem, though, for all the Adventist girls in the church were related to him. What could he do? Although his schooling had been scattered and he could hardly read, he decided to go to Hutchinson, Minnesota to attend the Danish-Norwegian Theological Seminary (which later became Maplewood Academy) with the hopes of finding a wife. His pursuit was successful.

She had dark and curly hair, hazel eyes, an inquisitive mind, and a teaching background.

Whenever she first stood up, she had a noticeable limp. Her name was Minnie Johnson; her family was Danish-German. She, too, had grown up on a farm, but in her family, education was a top priority. Her own mother was a school teacher. To properly educate the nine Johnson children, the family had moved to Hutchinson.

Her limp resulted from an accident when she was 14. Her father had been out hunting, and as he walked home, he played with a bullet. He put it into his pocket, then in the gun, then into his pocket. When he came home, he laid the gun on a bench near where the children were filling the wash tubs with water. Her brother picked up the gun, laid it across the tubs, and said, "Minnie, I'm going to shoot you."

Now Pa had never left the gun loaded before, so, without fear, she said, "Go ahead."

Minnie was sitting on a bench combing Duane's hair. There was a bang. The shot missed Duane's head, but hit her in the thigh. She was sick a long time. When confronted with the loss of her leg, she chose death. Fortunately, she survived, but she was never able to walk without pain again.

The Dan Johnson family about the time Dad and Mom were married.

Dad met Minnie on a Sabbath when he happened to walk by the Johnson home to meet with friends. He spotted Minnie and invited her to accompany him to "MV," the Missionary Volunteer meeting for youth. Their friendship grew, even though it was somewhat difficult for a dormitory student to visit a girl in the village. After some time, their romance blossomed into a life partnership.

In 1926, Dad brought his new bride back to Ruthven. For a time the newly-weds lived with Grandma and Grandpa Hansen. Minnie stated that her new mother-in-law was the most wonderful person she had ever known. Soon, though, Grandpa Hansen purchased a farm for Dad and Mom, as he did for all the boys when they reached manhood. They would all share-crop with him. This is how my parents set up housekeeping on the Ayrshire farm.

From the beginning the couple established a family altar. As Dad read the Bible verses, his reading skills increased until he could enjoy studying the Bible, Ellen White books, church papers, and farm journals.

Before the first child was born, the young couple made plans to move near a church school. Dad searched and found a good farm in the hills south of Ruthven to rent, but in making the final arrangements, the owner specified that Dad would need to grow hogs. Seventh-day Adventists are discouraged from eating pork. Dad could not conscientiously do this, so the deal was cancelled. Dad and Mom were sorely disappointed.

Howard and Minnie wedding portrait.

At Ayrshire, God blessed the couple with seven children—the six mentioned previously, plus another daughter, Grace. Five years after Grace, Mom went to the hospital for the birth of their eighth child. That boy, Ivan, completed the family circle.

As the children grew to school age, their schooling situation became more urgent. The year we all had the whooping cough, Stella lived with Grandpa and Grandma Hansen in Ruthven. When Stella was in the second grade, MaryEtta, the second daughter, was ready to start school. That year my parents decided to keep Stella at home, and she, along with MaryEtta, walked the two miles together to public school. The next year they were joined by the third sister, Rosy. The girls clearly remember the cold winters. They would stop at a neighbor's house to warm up on the way home and to eat the cookies she always had for them. Spring was much warmer, but the melting snow caused flooding of some roads. When the water was deep, Dad went with them to help them cross.

In 1937, the Ruthven church decided to start a church school. Today twelve miles does not seem far, but there were times when the snow made the road impassable. The spring rains and melting snow turned the dirt into mud, creating deep ruts where the cars and buggies drove. It was too difficult for our family to take the children every day to school.

What could they do?

Grandpa Hansen weighed the situation and resolved the problem. He purchased another farm on the northwest outskirts of Ruthven for our family and invited Dad's younger sister, Evelyn and her husband, Thomas, to move to our Ayrshire farm.

The new farm covered 113 acres, a bit smaller than Ayrshire, but the soil was richer.

The one-story house was small and inconvenient in many ways. There was a front porch that was more like a sunroom with windows all around. It was hot in the summer and cold in the winter. The living room had a colored-glass door leading to the porch. There was a

Ariel view of the Ruthven farm in later years.

dining room large enough to accommodate a large table with chairs and two bedrooms with a hallway leading to a trap-door that opened into the basement. The kitchen only had a few cupboards and a pump in the corner that provided rain-water from a cistern. There was an outside pump as well that provided all other water. Off the kitchen was another small room which opened onto the back porch. There was no electricity, no running water, and no bathroom. (There hadn't been any at Ayrshire either.) That was all there was to the house, but we were within easy walking distance of the new school, and that was all that mattered. This move was the first of many sacrifices Mom and Dad made to provide a Christian education for us.

Looking back, I feel blessed to have been born and raised in a secure, caring, devout Seventh-day Adventist home. I owe so much to the intentional, sacrificial, lifelong choices of my parents and extended family. The Lord was represented well by my earthly father and mother, a good farmer dressed in bib overalls and his beloved wife.

The little house.

CHAPTER 3
The Heart of My Inspiration

Personally, the move to Ruthven couldn't have been timed better. My developing mind was thirsty to experience a bigger world. After all, I was now four years old.

Wide-eyed, I watched as Mom nested our family of nine into the new farm house. The only way we fit was to limit our clothes, toys, and other "stuff." Mom and Dad claimed the smaller bedroom. There were two double beds in the second bedroom where four of us slept and a third double bed on the front porch where two of us slept. Lyle used a day bed in the living room. When Ivan was born, a crib was placed in the dining room. Electricity was soon put in, but it took some time for Mom to devise a way to add an indoor bathroom. Eventually, half of the small room off the kitchen served that purpose. Over time our parents made many other improvements to the house.

With the disorganization caused from our move, Mom rallied the teacher in her to marshal our tribe. Both Mom and Dad were determined that their children would be well-trained spiritually, mentally, physically, and socially. They also wanted to make sure that we knew how to work on a farm.

Because of these values, our day began with farm chores, including milking the cows. (The story is told that at one time Dad had a milking machine. Unfortunately, the girls began squabbling in the evening, and Mom requested Dad to sell the milking machine so the children would have something productive to do.) Chores completed, we ate breakfast, usually hot cereal, milk, cream, bread, and canned fruit.

After the meal chairs were pushed back, and Dad took out his Bible while Mom retrieved the Sabbath school quarterly. We sat quietly while the lesson was read and then Dad would pray. It was amazing to hear Dad pray. Usually, he was a quiet man who had difficulty expressing himself; he let others do the talking. But when he prayed, he became fluent. His strong relationship with God seemed to free his speech.

During the school year, we were expected to have the milking done, dishes washed, beds made, and house swept before we went to school. In the evening after school, we were each assigned chores both in the house and outside. For our evening inside job, we normally helped prepare the evening meal. Our outside job involved the chickens. There were two hen houses and water had to be pumped from the well and carried in buckets to both. After that the eggs had to be gathered. This was a pleasant job when the weather was nice, but it was not so enjoyable when the rain poured down or a winter storm raged.

These tasks were followed by the evening meal, study of the children's Sabbath school lesson, then milking the cows again. Mom's main concern was that each child needed to learn how to do everything, so the assignments were rotated. In the summer we often helped Dad with his farm work. Bedtime came fairly early. I very much disliked going to bed in the summer when the sun was still up.

The chores in winter caused me some grief. At ten years old, I went through a rapid growth spurt, achieving my present height within a year. It took a long time for my coordination to catch up with my changing body. The pump where I filled the buckets was near the barn, and the chicken houses were farther beyond. Ice seemed to develop every year on the path at the corner of the barn where I had to walk. Invariably, I fell on the ice with those buckets of water skinning my knees and thighs. Nevertheless, the job had to be done, so it was back to the pump for two more buckets of water. How did I manage to make the second trip successfully? I don't remember, but I do recall having bruises all winter. How delicious it felt to return to the house and stand over the hot register in the dining room, which was heated by a large coal-burning furnace in the basement. Despite the pleasure the warmth gave us, we had to be careful not to let our shoes get too hot or they would begin to melt.

Before Sabbath began we bathed, cleaned the house, and prepared food. On Friday evenings during the long winter, Mom would read whole books to us at a time. The Sabbath was welcomed with joy. On Sabbath morning the Howard Hansen family headed for the little white church with tall, colored-glass windows. The wooden-structure consisted of a sanctuary with long unpadded pews. A large roll-down door closed off the back portion for a children's Sabbath school room. All of the children met together in this one room. A bookcase full of books was on one side, a pump organ on the other. After Sabbath school, the door was raised and the previously closed-off room became part of the sanctuary. A large furnace in the basement sent hot air up through the register near the roll-down door. We often congregated around the register before and after services. The outhouse was out back. Grandpa Hansen lived next-door to the church, so our family usually used their indoor bathroom. Much later, the church basement was enlarged, an oil heater was installed, bathrooms were put in, and the children's department was moved downstairs.

Second in importance to worship and spiritual instruction was Christian education. Dad helped build the church school, and he always contributed heavily to it financially. The school was built of wood and consisted of an entry hallway and a large classroom that had windows all along one side where one teacher taught grades 1 through 10. In the back there was a smaller room that served as a library as well as a second classroom when one was needed. Outhouses were out back. Later a basement with restrooms was added there, too. We played in the basement when the weather prevented us from going outside. A playground with poles for a volleyball net completed the school. Fortunately, the school was adjacent to the public school baseball diamond. In the winter we made a large circle for playing fox and geese there. In the summer it made a good place to play dare base, softball, and many other games.

School programs were important church social events. We practiced for weeks to prepare music programs, skits, readings, and whatever else our teacher planned. The desks were moved to make room for the "stage," and a curtain of sheets was hung to give the student performers time to get ready. All the students were included in the programs. It was fun as well as a learning diversion from our usual studies.

Usually, I was the only student in my class, though sometimes I joined classes with the next grade up. As the only student in that particular grade, I received relatively little attention from the busy teacher who taught all the grades. Fortunately, I was a self-starter, but it did get a little lonely. This resulted in a limited development of social skills. Instead, I read. I read most of the books in the school library, including the encyclopedias and all of the books in the church library. Many of them were about missionaries.

Mom also took us to the county library. How vividly I remember those trips. It was cool, very quiet, and had the odor of slightly moldy, old books. We could quietly walk around the shelves and read the titles of the books. I found it to be a fascinating place. Each of us soon found our favorite sections and checked out the books we wanted to read.

The depression had a long-term impact on our family. Money was scarce. We ate primarily garden produce. Mom never fully recovered from the concern of not having sufficient money. My parent's motto became, "Live very frugally." In addition, they believed that their resources were lent to them by God, and they should use them wisely and return a generous portion to the Lord. As soon as we children were eleven or twelve years old, we were expected to help financially. We took whatever jobs were available—house cleaning, babysitting, clerking in the drug store, farm work, or detasseling corn. Ruthven was home to the DeKalb Seed Company. Anyone willing to work met their truck on a corner in Ruthven and was driven to their fields. Two kinds of corn had been planted in alternate rows. We had to pull all the tassels out of the corn in part of the rows so the pollination worked right. We came home at nights with sunburns and cold sores.

Aside from the routine, we found time to play. There were a number of other children in the neighborhood, so we played group games. The games did not require expensive equipment, but we had fun. We did not generally have toys owned by one person. Except for a few small items, the toys were owned by all. Paper dolls were cut out of old catalogues from Montgomery Ward and Sears and Roebuck. In the winter we built snow forts and igloos, had snowball fights, and made angels in the snow.

Music was also important. There was usually only enough money for one of us to take piano lessons, but eventually most of us had some lessons. We took turns practicing. When two or three wanted to play at the same time, we would sit and watch the person at the piano. Whenever the player looked at the keys, it was the next person's turn to play! There was no begging us to practice; it was a privilege. Mom also taught us to sing old songs that I have never heard elsewhere.

The Hansen family now complete.

After that bad winter when we were all sick, there was seldom illness in the family. Mom took care of what sicknesses or injuries we had, administering hot foot baths for upper respiratory infections. Doctor visits were rare, except for Mom's pregnancies. Even injuries were patched up unless she thought there might be a fracture. She also applied her medical knowledge to the livestock. She did difficult deliveries of the calves and treated infections that cows and horses periodically had. With her practical knowledge and feeding us a wholesome diet to the best of her knowledge, she kept us healthy.

One of the things we did not like in winter was the long underwear and cotton stockings that always seemed to sag and bag and were uncomfortable. We had to wear them until the temperature reached 60 degrees. Much to the horror of Grandma Johnson, Mom finally allowed us to scrap them. Grandma was sure that we would die of pneumonia. Instead of the long underwear and stockings, we wore ski pants when we went outside in cold weather.

I prospered under this program. I was healthy. I learned how to work. I gained basic life skills, and I loved to read. At age eleven I learned to know Jesus as a friend, as Someone who was interested in me personally, and as Someone who was my powerful protector. No longer did I attend church just because it was expected of me; instead, I was doing something I wanted to do. With this new relationship with Jesus, I chose to be baptized into the Seventh-day Adventist Church, something I never regretted. It is interesting that at a time when many taught legalism, I saw the Ten Commandments as a protection, and the seventh-day Sabbath as a pleasure. My siblings did not all see it that way.

Like the roots of a tall tree, the foundations of my life were put in place during my grade school years. They were the product of the purposeful efforts of my parents and their allies—teachers, pastors, friends, and family. As I reviewed my childhood later in life, it surprised me to discover how much four men in my family also influenced my life: Uncle Ted, Uncle Dale, Uncle Duane, and Grandpa Johnson.

Uncle Ted was one of Dad's younger brothers living in Ruthven. Besides being a likable uncle, he fascinated me because he only had one leg. As I grew older, I learned he had lost his leg in a tractor accident. Somehow, he was thrown between a tractor wheel and the equipment he was pulling. The tractor kept running in a circle until a neighbor managed to jump on and stop it. His leg was twisted off at the thigh. However, he found a way to live life as though he had two legs. In time, his example of dealing with his disability would become an anchor in my life.

The Martin Hansen family before the deaths of 3 son.

Soon after we moved to the Ruthven farm, Uncle Dale, Dad's youngest brother became sick. He was a fine-looking high school senior. We loved his kind, gentle, personable ways. Grandpa and Grandma Hansen were so proud of him. The night after he went with his high school class to get senior pictures taken, he went to bed, never to go to school again, for he was very ill. He became sicker and sicker. At the time Grandpa and Grandma Hansen happened to be away in Minnesota. They made plans to come home at once, but a blizzard roared in, which made travel impossible for several days.

Mom spent much time caring for Dale, as did his sisters, but he did not improve. By the time Grandpa and Grandma Hansen arrived, he was very sick, with an ineffective doctor treating him. No matter what treatment was given, it had no effect because he had a kidney problem known as Bright's Disease, now known as nephritis. Dialysis was not yet available. On my fifth birthday, Uncle Dale died.

There was weeping, yes, but there was no hysteria or wailing. The funeral was large because most of the people in town knew him. Life went on, but even as a young child, I sensed Grandpa and Grandma Hansen's hurt. In fact, the whole family did. Grandma kept Dale's senior picture in a prominent place in the house. Later I learned that Dale was the fourth son Grandpa and Grandma had buried. Of course, they also carried sorrow from Ted's loss in the tractor accident. This was an education in the reality of life, and I also found it to be instructive on what was an acceptable display of grief in my Danish culture.

The next "training" I had in handling grief was when we received a phone call from Hutchinson, Minnesota, which carried the news that my other grandpa—Grandpa Johnson—had died. The message stated that Grandpa's heart had stopped beating in his sleep. Grandpa Johnson had particularly endeared himself to me one fall day when I found myself tangled in an argument with my namesake, the spinster Aunt Sadie, mother's oldest sister. Aunt Sadie decided I should recite my memory verse to her, and I decided I would not. So, I didn't. (Aunt Sadie had previously voiced her opinion to my mother that my strong will needed to be broken. Mother responded that I would need that strong will to get me through difficult times in life.) Well, when I didn't say my memory verse, Aunt Sadie exiled me outdoors and said, "Iris, you can come back in when you are ready to say that memory verse."

Grandpa Johnson, learning of my plight, took my hand, led me around the house to the back door, and let me in. So, when Grandpa Johnson died, I felt the loss of a true ally. Again, I noticed that when our family received the news of his death, and also at the funeral, there was no loud crying or wailing, only controlled sobbing.

Duane and Shirley, waiting to go to Burma, with brother Kimber and wife Helen.

The other uncle who powerfully influenced my life was Uncle Duane, Mom's younger brother. Fortunately, he did not give me another lesson in grief. Newly married to Aunt Shirley, the couple accepted a mission appointment to Burma in 1941. The newlyweds prepared their shipment and had it loaded on the boat that they themselves anticipated boarding. However, with World War II simmering, international relations were tense, and Uncle Duane and Aunt Shirley were not allowed to board the ship. Their belongings made the trip all the way to Burma and back. The second time they attempted to go overseas, Uncle Duane and Aunt Shirley were able to go. They went to Rangoon and started language study with plans to go into more active mission service when that was finished. However, when the Japanese took over the Burma Road, they were evacuated and were only able to take out a suitcase or two. They were reassigned to work in Pakistan and India where they worked many years. Every furlough, I listened eagerly to stories of their adventures. This, along with the many mission books I had read, made me determined that someday I would be a missionary.

Chapter 4

God Stands at the Fork in the Road

In our family we children attended Seventh-day Adventist schools; we did that from grade school through college. Our local Ruthven church school took us through the tenth grade. After that, one-by-one we ventured off to academy, then to college. Our parents supported us as far as we wished to go. We all worked as much as possible, but the tremendous financial burden fell on Mom and Dad. They wore the same clothes, drove the same car, and scrimped in many other areas of their life to make our education happen.

One's teenage years are always a challenge, but they are also a time of learning and growing. I found that by daily surrendering to Jesus, He was somehow able to navigate me through the maze of options life presented. How had God led me? I didn't hear Him speak, but later as I reminisced, it became obvious that God had influenced the decisions I made, even those that seemed inconsequential at the time. Many of those choices I prayed about; others I didn't. Although I was young and naive, there were many times that God kept me from making disastrous moves that would harm me.

By the time I was ready for the tenth grade, the number of students at the Ruthven school had decreased; and since I was again the only student in the class, my parents decided I needed a new environment. I was not consulted, but I certainly agreed! I had sisters at Oak Park Academy in Nevada, Iowa, and at Maplewood Academy in Hutchinson, Minnesota, (where Dad met Mom). Both these were schools were Seventh-day Adventist boarding schools. Stella was at Union College in Nebraska; MaryEtta and Rosy both graduated that year and continued on to Union College. My parents decided that Shirley and I should attend Maplewood. Education has been a strong feature of the Seventh-day Adventist Church. To accommodate the membership, boarding schools had been established for high school and college level students.

Except for Ivan, we are all teenagers or older.

As a new sophomore, I was a shy bookworm that desperately needed to learn social graces. Opportunity for friendships had been limited in our little town. Being the fifth girl, I felt like an ugly duckling. My older sisters were talented, beautiful, and brainy. It seemed God had run out of gifts when He came to me. How could I survive? Would I fit? Could I succeed? I was afraid. However, having read the book *Christ's Object Lessons*, I was comforted with the thought that everybody—even an awkward girl from a farm in Iowa—had at least one talent.

But I need not have worried, for soon I was part of a circle of friends my own age. Fortunately, the friends I found were spiritually minded and excellent students. We challenged each other scholastically. We studied together, sang in the choir together, played in the orchestra together, prayed together, and played together. I loved it, and I am glad to say that those friendships endure to this day.

All of us worked as much as we could to earn our way through the academy. When I was a junior, I was a reader for the Bible teacher (a reader corrects papers, keeps records, etc.) and my sister, Shirley, worked in the book bindery. I received the top student wages, 45 cents an hour. When the government implemented minimum wages, the schools had to pay those who worked in the industries accordingly. Shirley was paid almost double what I received. Those students did not complain, but the rest of us weren't so sure this was fair.

I was introduced to city life when Shirley and I visited MaryEtta's home. MaryEtta worked in the "loop," as downtown Minneapolis was called. Having grown up in a Scandinavian/German community, it amazed and interested me to see the variety of people living in the city. It was the first time I had ever seen an African-American, as well as people of other nationalities. Just the number of people and cars amazed me. MaryEtta warned us that we had to be much more cautious in the city, as it was not as safe as the country. We had to remember to always lock our cars and homes in the city, something we never did back home.

Attending Maplewood gave Shirley and me opportunities to become better acquainted with Mom's family, especially the cousins who attended Maplewood at the same time that we did. Sometimes on Sabbaths we were invited to one of their homes. We enjoyed being with family and appreciated taking breaks from the routine of school.

The colporteur leader for the Minnesota Conference visited the academy and encouraged students to canvass for the summer. Canvassing was when people went door-to-door selling religious books. Three of us decided to accept the challenge. The leader took us to Minneapolis and told us where to work. Briefly he taught us how to sell books. To my disappointment, I was a total failure as a salesperson. When people told me they liked the books, but didn't have money to buy them, I believed them. I knew what it was like to not have money. Consequently, the sales didn't close. It was an education for me. Though the adventure was a financial disaster, I learned from that experience that I could quite easily mingle with strangers.

Shirley graduated when I was a junior. After finishing Maplewood, it was popular to go to Emmanuel Missionary College (now Andrews University) in Michigan rather than to Union College. Shirley chose EMC. She described the beautiful campus in the country with its new brick girl's dorm and an "avenue" of grass and trees that gave the campus an organized, park-like appearance. It sounded attractive.

During my last year, we seniors spent many happy hours discussing which college we would attend and what major we would take. On college day the Maplewood Seniors were taken to Union College, to encourage us to attend there. Union had been built on a farm in the country, but over the years, much of the land was sold in order to fund the school, so the city of Lincoln enveloped the college. A major street ran by the campus. The old wooden buildings were unappealing to me. I compared it to Shirley's description of Emmanuel Missionary College. Even though many of my relatives had chosen Union, none of them would be there the next year. Several of my classmates had decided to go to EMC rather than to Union, so I joined them.

Graduation from academy was a big event met with mixed emotions. It meant saying goodbye to classmates and faculty, many of whom I would never see again. Maplewood had been my home-away-from-home for three years. These people had been my family. Though sad, graduation was also a joyful time of looking forward to exciting, new experiences.

To earn money for college, I worked in Minneapolis that summer at the same office where MaryEtta worked. The job was mostly office work, and it reinforced my interest in becoming a secretary or possibly a bookkeeper. I admired my mother who was first a wife and mother, and secondly, a professional woman. Unfortunately for me, my lack of confidence made marriage seem remote. I figured I would go into mission service as a single person like so many others had done.

That fall, Mom, MaryEtta, and Bud (MaryEtta's husband) drove me to EMC to start a new life on a strange campus. Shirley had sparked the interest in my decision of attending EMC, but she was teaching that year rather than attending college, so for the first time in my life, I was away from all of my immediate family.

Registration at EMC forced some career decisions. What was I going to take? I considered taking biology or archaeology, but I wondered how I would earn money in those fields. My goal was to serve the Lord in mission service, and neither of those majors seemed to fit that bill. My experience in Minneapolis and at academy working for the Bible teacher caused me to favor a secretarial course. Stella had taken nursing at Union College. Perhaps nursing would be a good choice for me also? To help us make the choice, students were given aptitude tests. This should have helped me make the decision, but I scored equally in secretarial and nursing!

Graduation is also decision time. Which college should I attend?

Praying over what I should take brought no direction. Finally, the decision was made to take courses that would keep my options open. I would enroll both in secretarial courses and add as many pre-nursing subjects as possible. In another year, after I had completed all the prerequisites needed for both, I would finally come to a decision.

The next spring as I was making plans for the summer, surprise! An opportunity opened up that no one expected. Representatives from Hinsdale Sanitarium and Hospital in Illinois arrived on campus with an offer. Because the buildings at Hinsdale were in need of repairs, Hinsdale was in the midst of an extensive building program. The result was a decreased enrollment in the nursing school. As was typical, nursing students were needed to help staff the hospital. Without the students, the hospital would be in trouble.

A little research at EMC revealed that a number of us had followed a plan similar to mine. We had taken anatomy and physiology but not chemistry and microbiology. The representatives from Hinsdale arranged to teach these two classes during the summer, and they offered the pre-nursing students the following proposal: Any student who would take these two classes in the summer, thus completing the pre-nursing requirements, and would enroll at Hinsdale in the fall, would have their tuition, food, and lodging paid for during the summer. In addition, Hinsdale would waive the usual registration fee. Wow! To financially strapped students, this sounded like manna from heaven! Several of us accepted their offer, including three of my academy classmates. My career decision was cemented. I would become a nurse. Had I wasted my time taking secretarial courses? Over time, my secretarial skills would prove to be useful.

Hinsdale's plan offered financial benefits beyond the special offer they presented to us as pre-nursing students. Being a diploma school, rather than a four-year bachelor program like Union, I could earn most of my way through college. I would also gain additional practical nursing experience not so attainable in the four-year program. The down-side was that I could not earn a bachelor's degree by the end of the program, which was something I would someday want.

If I had decided on nursing as the career of choice for me when I was an academy senior, I may have chosen Union instead. The difference in cost would have been considerable. In a collegiate program, regular college tuition must be paid throughout the full four years. This would have been a heavy burden for me and for my parents. As it turned out, my parents didn't have to pay anything for my nursing education, which made me very happy.

Looking back, I'm amazed at the times when a seemingly simple choice was made when the alternative could have majorly changed the outcome of my life. When I went away to boarding school, my parents could easily have chosen Oak Park Academy rather than Maplewood. The distance from home was about the same. When it came time for college, it did not seem like a significant decision to attend EMC rather than Union. Would I have taken nursing if I had gone to Union? What would my life have been like if I had chosen Oak Park and Union? We can't go back and relive those years to find out, but the choices I made did determine my future, and I believe God led in those choices. Through these experiences, I've come to believe that for His precious children, God stands at every fork in the road.

Chapter 5
In the Days of My Youth

Summer school at EMC passed quickly, and we soon found ourselves at Hinsdale, enrolled in their three-year diploma nursing program. We started as apprehensive "probationers." Probation was a time when we took introductory courses, like nursing arts, and learned how to do morning and evening patient care. It was a time when the students could decide whether or not they really wanted to be nurses, and a time when the faculty could decide whether or not we had the aptitude for nursing. Over those three months, none of us changed our minds, and the faculty decided we could all make it. The school then inducted us into the nursing profession with a special capping ceremony.

The cap and uniform quickly informed both patients and staff of our student status. The uniform consisted of a blue and white striped cotton "dress" with stiffly starched cuffs and collar, a starched apron, white shoes, white stockings, and the all-important cap. When on duty, we were never to appear without full uniform. A navy and red wool cape warmed us in winter. Our uniforms signified achievement, and we wore them with pride.

Our caps had no stripes during our first year (our sophomore year in college). Juniors added one black stripe on the corner of the cap, and seniors added an additional stripe. Graduate nurses wore white uniforms with the school pin and no stripe on the cap until they passed state boards. Registered nurses wore one black narrow stripe on the full width of the cap. Supervisors wore a cap with two narrow, full-width stripes. The director of nurses wore a cap with a wide blue stripe across the full width of the cap.

Hinsdale was a suburb of Chicago. At the time many millionaires lived there. The shops offered wildly expensive shoes, clothes, and more. It was fun to look but not to buy. The streets were tree-lined, the homes ostentatious, the yards beautifully landscaped and meticulously kept. On pleasant days when schedules permitted, I liked to walk through the residential area. It gave me time to meditate and to sort out life.

To reach the hospital, you crossed railroad tracks via a bridge. Originally, the hospital had been a resort. Built for the wealthy, the building had been impressive and perhaps a little ornate. Now it was old and had been modified a number of times to make it a well-functioning hospital. The campus included not only the hospital, but an impressive stone church, and staff housing. A circular driveway led to the front entrance of the hospital. On the right was the wing that housed the female students. (I don't remember where the male students lived.) In the center was the long hospital building, and on the left was the newer brick addition to the hospital. Because these were all attached, it was not necessary for us to go outside when the weather was inclement.

Nursing school presented many challenges academically, socially, and spiritually. Working together, studying together, and playing together, we students soon felt like a family. Our days were portioned between work and classes. When there were staff shortages in the hospital, the student nurses were employed. At those times the hours stretched long, but through it all, we learned how to work as part of a team.

We were confronted with the joys and sorrows of our patients. The sorrows were often difficult. One of my patients was a cancer patient. Part of her colon had been removed which necessitated a surgical colostomy (they surgically formed an artificial anus). How does a healthy, 20-year-old student nurse relate to that? Moreover, after this patient returned home, she went out to burn the trash and fainted, falling forward into the fire. Third-degree burns covered her abdomen, as well as other parts of her body. The excruciating pain, the discouragement, and the horror of what had happened overwhelmed her. In addition to the difficult emotional and physical care of this patient, the odor was almost overpowering. After suffering many weeks, she died. It was a challenging learning experience for me.

While I was at Hinsdale, a polio epidemic raged through the country. One day a person could be healthy and active, and then within a day or two, he could be completely paralyzed. The most debilitating type was the bulbar polio. This type of polio affected one's ability to breathe. These patients were placed in an iron lung that helped them breathe. The whole body was encased; only the head remained outside. Nursing care was given through portholes. To help us understand what the patients felt like in that confined space, each student nurse spent time inside the iron lung.

Polio was especially traumatic for sports-minded teenagers and young parents. Hinsdale Sanitarium and Hospital became well-known in the area for its treatment of polio patients. The large hydrotherapy and rehabilitation department was kept busy treating the after-effects of acute polio. We students became a part of that rehab team. With treatment, many of the patients recovered enough to walk again. Some left the hospital to face a life in wheelchairs or in a wheelchair equipped with portable respirators. What trauma those people experienced, as did we in caring for them! Those encounters forced us to face the realities of life. The chaplain, faculty, and experienced RNs were always a source of counseling. However, even with counseling, the process of dealing with pain, suffering, and death was emotionally painful to us students. There always seemed to be patients who were especially difficult. Fortunately, there were others who recovered quickly and soon went home. The student nurses, including myself, didn't always do well, but we were learning not only the technicalities of nursing, but also the psychological aspects. These were lessons I would need later in life.

There are many serious aspects of nursing, but as nursing students, we were also typical young people in our late teens and early twenties. One of the ways we students relieved the stress of the sorrows was with laughter. As is common in many nursing schools, the "probies" (beginning students on "probation") are the target of jokes. Yes, when we were still the probies, one of us (I don't remember which one) was sent to central supply to get a fallopian tube (a pair of tubes that carries the egg from the ovary to the uterus of a woman). Of course, the workers in central supply played along with the pranksters and sent the student to the operating room to find it. To the juniors who instigated the "fun," it was hilarious. To the student who went searching to find the tube, it was not. Of course, the new students never forgot the name of this piece of human anatomy.

Another prank was to give a fellow nursing student a drink which contained a certain dye that turned the urine red. The unwitting student would then go to the clinic because they believed there was blood in his or her urine.

Some of our laughs came from unexpected happenings while caring for patients. In our group some students were tall and some were very short. Joan was a jolly, short nurse, and on one particular day, she was assigned a grossly obese patient. Since she could not reach across the lady, she had to bathe one side of the body, then move the equipment to the other side of the bed and bathe that side. Back in the dorm, Joan told her experience with such animation that we all had to laugh.

Then there was the problem with the Alka-Seltzer. Fellow-nurse Bob was unacquainted with this stomach remedy. On the medicine card, the orders said to give Mr. Z. two Alka-Seltzers. Bob looked at the pills and thought, "Those are pretty big pills to swallow, but Mr. Z. is also pretty big." Obediently, he put the pills in his mouth and gave him some water. Immediately, the pills began to fizz, and bubbles came out of Mr. Z's mouth. Bob quickly realized his error—the pills should have been dissolved in a glass of water *before* giving them to the patient. Bob was so embarrassed that he hastily left the room and asked a classmate to trade patients with him for the remainder of the shift, so he would not have to face the patient again. We all enjoyed Bob's misery because it could have happened to any one of us.

Changes were happening at the hospital as well as in our personal lives. The new buildings were rapidly going up. A new dormitory was built across the street adjacent to the church. Our class was among the first to occupy that building with its pleasant lobby and worship room. There was new furniture in each room. (What was not quite as agreeable was the list of room-use regulations the faculty presented to us, but we adjusted.) The planners thoughtfully made a tunnel under the street from the dormitory to the hospital. Besides serving as a place to run the heating pipes and utility lines, the students could use the tunnel to walk between buildings without having to go outside. It was a big day for us when the hospital moved into the new brick structure and the old wooden buildings were demolished.

The downtown Chicago commuter train ran through Hinsdale on the track next to the hospital. To board it, we needed to walk into Hinsdale to the station. For entertainment, a group of us would sometimes ride the train to the big city and window shop. We treated the stores like museums—"look only"—as we didn't really have much money to purchase anything. It was a fun break from the routine to see what was going on in the rest of the world.

To complete our education, the nursing school arranged affiliations in pediatrics, mental health, and communicable diseases. A hospital vehicle took some of us to Detroit to the children's hospital for our pediatric affiliation. While we were there, we mixed with students from other nursing schools. At one time the pediatric hospital had been in a good neighborhood, but now it was in the red-light district and was dangerous. If we needed to go the hospital after sundown, we had to stop at the police station and have them take us back. This was a new environment for us. At times, dealing with so many sick children was overtaxing. It frightened us, for we knew so little and had so much responsibility. Many of the children came from very poor homes where the parents had few resources to care for their children. Many children also came from divided homes. We were overburdened with the sadness in the world.

The state mental hospital in Illinois was another draining experience. We were the first students to go there, so this was an uncertain experience both for the mental hospital and for us. There they divided the patients into those who were considered treatable and those who were deemed not treatable. The latter just received basic care for their needs. After spending time there, I became confident that psychiatric nursing was not for me.

As state boards and graduation drew near, it was time to plan our immediate futures. I opted to work at Hinsdale for a few months until the results of state boards arrived.

Graduation was an exciting occasion. Finally, it was time for us to shed out of our student uniforms

Now a graduate nurse, but the stripe waited until state boards were passed.

and don white ones to march down the aisle of the church. Family members arrived to witness this solemn event. The speakers challenged us to represent both our nursing profession and Christ. I was thrilled to think that God had my destiny in His hands. I purposed to do my best in order to prepare myself for His service.

What would our futures hold? Would we ever again see those who were going elsewhere to work? We praised the Lord that He had seen us through the past three years. We realized how different we were from the probationers who wondered only three years ago if we could succeed in the nursing profession. Now we were confident graduates, ready to take our places in the medical world, but first we had to pass our state nursing boards.

In order to accomplish this, we went into Chicago for two days of answering multiple-choice questions in each area of nursing. After that, we had to survive the weeks of waiting for the results. Only those who have waited weeks and weeks to learn the results of an important test can understand the anxiety we experienced. Had we passed? Had we passed some sections, but not others? What must we do if we hadn't? Finally, the all-important letters came. Yeah! We all passed! Now we were full-fledged registered nurses and could plan our long-term futures.

At the time there were two goals I had for my professional life: I wished to have experience in a small hospital, and I wanted to complete more education. By now I realized that it was wise to obtain a college BS degree to keep up with developments in the nursing profession.

To accomplish the first goal, I contacted Stella, my oldest sister who was living in Fruita, Colorado. I had visited there once and loved the mountains near Fruita. Stella was married and practiced nursing in a small hospital there. One November morning, after having worked the night before, I was sound asleep when the phone rang. Groggily, I answered. It was my sister, Shirley, phoning from Plentywood, Montana with a request. The hospital there was very short of nurses. Would I come there to work? Go to Montana in December? Shirley assured me that the single staff lived downstairs in the hospital, so I wouldn't need to go out in the cold and snow unless I wanted to. She also mentioned that the Adventist church was just across the street. I decided to go to Montana until June. After that, I planned to go to Walla Walla College (now Walla Walla University) in Washington state to complete my college degree.

How different Plentywood's hospital was from Hinsdale! The departments at Plentywood were consolidated. The nurse on duty was expected to handle the medical surgical unit and obstetrics—including the delivery room and emergency room. It was a good experience, but being on night duty alone was not something I would want to do again. It convinced me that two people should always be on duty each and every shift.

As summer came, it was now time to pursue my second goal. For this degree, I decided to pursue my interest in biology by taking electives in that field. One of the attractions for going to Walla Walla College was their biology station located on the Puget Sound near Anacortes. So, I was soon off to Seattle where Dr. Booth met me at the airport. As we drove to Anacortes, he introduced me to the joys of biology. For this student from the plains of Iowa, the biology station was exhilarating. The ocean and mountains, the spectacular scenery of the northwest, as well as being able to observe entirely new birds and other wild life, made this a special summer. I loved the ocean. The creatures in the sea fascinated me. But boating was another matter, especially in stormy weather. Motion sickness plagued me which made some trips uncomfortable.

In the fall I moved to the main Walla Walla campus. The first order of business was to take a National League of Nursing examination to assure the college that it was safe to give me credit from the nursing program at Hinsdale. I successfully passed. What followed was a busy year filled with classes and college life. Since I was already an RN and understood concepts from that viewpoint, I found my nursing classes at Walla Walla quite different from those I had taken as a beginning student at Hinsdale. As a number of my classmates were RNs from other diploma schools, it was interesting to share experiences from the various hospitals.

There was also the major adjustment of living in a college dormitory. At Hinsdale, the philosophy of the faculty was that since we were now responsible for patient's lives, we should also be responsible for our own. Rules were relatively few. After graduation, there had been no rules, for I lived in an apartment with classmates. In Montana, the hospital provided living quarters, and my roommates were not Adventists. When I came to Walla Walla College, it didn't occur to me to get an apartment in College Place. So, if I were to live in a college dormitory, I must bow to the rules. It was difficult at first. Fortunately, I had never owned a car, so I had not become accustomed to that freedom. But I adjusted, and in the end, I enjoyed the experience.

One day, there was a letter in my mailbox from the General Conference (GC), the world headquarters of the Seventh-day Adventist Church, inviting me to accept a position as an instructor in the school of nursing at the Adventist hospital in Rangoon, Burma. Would I be interested in going? Yes, of course, after I completed my education at Walla Walla College. My degree would be a bachelor's in nursing education, so I would be qualified to teach nursing. Excited that my dreams were becoming a reality so quickly, I responded at once with a positive answer. They sent back instructions to have a physical and begin the necessary immunizations. They also sent a passport application form with instructions for getting passport pictures taken. This made the appointment a reality. I could hardly believe it—I was truly going to the part of world of which I had read many stories about, even to the country where Uncle Duane had first been assigned. Burma was a fascinating land, and I began reading even more books about it.

I had saved money for college while working at Hinsdale and Montana, and I worked at Walla Walla General Hospital as much as my classes would allow, but in January it became obvious that my money would not last the year. What was I going to do? I didn't want to ask my parents for help. Amazingly, the Lord had a surprise in store for me. Dr. Hansen, chair of the nursing school, received an unexpected letter from the government. The U.S. government was very interested in nurses obtaining bachelor's degrees and had appropriated funding to assist student nurses with tuition and living expenses. The money had been appropriated before the school year, but not enough nurses had applied, so there was a surplus. The letter stated that this money was available only to nurses who came from states that did not offer a program where RNs could earn a bachelor's degree. Montana did not did not have any such programs, and I had just worked in Montana. This could be the answer to my financial concerns. Wow! If I had gone to Colorado rather than to Montana, I would not have qualified for this opportunity! I applied and was accepted.

The money allotted, however, was for *two* quarters. By the time I was accepted, I only had *one* quarter left to graduate. I originally had planned to return to my parent's home in Iowa after graduation so I could prepare to go to Burma, but since there was enough money available to support two quarters, why not begin my master's degree and then go home? It didn't seem like any major change in plans. I had not heard from the GC for some time, and I had no indication how long it might be before the visa could be obtained. I figured the more education I could get, the better prepared I would be. So, I registered to take practice teaching the first part of the summer on the main campus, and take more biology classes at the biology station during the second part of the summer.

Eventually, all the projects were completed and tests had been taken. It was time for another graduation, but this time it was for my bachelor's degree in nursing. Once again, graduation gave me a sense of accomplishment, excitement for the future, and sadness over saying goodbye to friends. It was an impressive weekend that was both solemn and fun. Most of my classmates were leaving, and here I was staying on campus to face the challenges of teaching senior nursing students and taking summer classes.

The evening of graduation I joined a group of students who were eating supper on the lawn. A couple of fellows joined us; they invited a friend and me to share the evening with them. That is when I met Dick Hayden.

Chapter 6

God's Footprints are in the Shadows

Dick Hayden had planned to leave on graduation day to fish in Alaska, but the owner of the boat notified him that the boat was not ready to go, so fishing for the summer was cancelled. Instead, Dick decided to stay in Walla Walla and work in the pea harvest. In the evenings he took groups of students in his blue and white station wagon to the swimming pool and to other fun places. When it was time for me to go to the biology station at Anacortes, he offered to take me. In order to be able to visit Anacortes often, he found a job in Tacoma and made weekend trips to the biology station. By the end of the summer, he proposed that we get married and go into mission service as a couple rather than singly. Now that was a major shift in my plans!

Who was this Dick Hayden? He had medium brown hair, freckles, and was about my height (5' 8"). He had grown up in Peru with his missionary parents. He had attended Walla Walla College, graduating with a major in industrial arts. He sang beautifully, played a mean trumpet, and enjoyed listening to his large collection of music records. He loved to tell stories and do pantomimes. He was athletic and liked to tumble—he could even walk down stairs on his hands. Dick was also a pilot. He and four of his college friends had purchased a plane together so they could all use it to learn to fly. (They sold the plane after graduation.) Dick's goal in life was to enter the mission service someday.

His proposal came after we had been acquainted less than three months. Was this what the Lord wanted me to

Dick Hayden

do? Some friends said, "Of course, get married." Others said, "You haven't known him long enough; you had better continue with your plans to go overseas." Believe me, this was a special time of consulting with the Lord! Once I had the assurance that the Lord would approve, I said, "Yes!" to Dick. Rather than go home to prepare for Burma, I went home to prepare for a September wedding. I wrote to the GC of the change in my life and of our willingness to go as a family. Interestingly, Burma soon became a communist country which was renamed "Myanmar," and the Adventist hospital in Rangoon was no more.

So, how had seemingly unimportant decisions affected this period of my life? If I had chosen to work those few months after Hinsdale anywhere other than Montana, I would not have qualified for the scholarship. If I had gone home for the summer, rather than staying in Walla Walla, I would never have met Dick. As far as Dick was concerned, he had not planned to be in Walla Walla for the summer either, but he adjusted his plans when the fishing boat was not ready to go to Alaska. Was this just happenstance? We didn't think so. We believed the Lord had brought us together for a purpose. Again, I had witnessed God standing at the forks in my road.

What fun I had making plans for our wedding in the little country church in Ruthven, Iowa. Dick's brother, Jack, and sister, Carolyn, were at Walla Walla, as well as my classmate, Frances, and Stan, a friend and violinist. It was finally decided that since Dick had a station wagon, he would bring all of them to Iowa. After the wedding, we planned to take them all back to Walla Walla. I boarded the bus to Grand Junction, Colorado to meet my parents who were visiting my sister, Stella, in Fruita. I rode home with them and began sewing my wedding dress and the bridesmaids' dresses.

Iris, Dick and Mother Hayden.

The day before the wedding we got a real surprise. Dick's parents, missionaries in Peru, had been on furlough the very year I had been at Walla Walla. (I had heard them give talks and tell stories in their Peruvian costumes; I had seen Elder Hayden's long snake skin; I had read *From Football Field to Mission Field,* the book written about Elder Hayden; but I had not met them personally.) They had returned to Lima, Peru in the spring, just a few months before, so it seemed impossible for them to return Stateside for the wedding. But Dick's mother could not miss this important event in her son's life, so she decided to fly up for the wedding anyway. From the airport she boarded a bus for a nearby station. On the way she phoned to let us know she was coming. That call came when Dick and I were not in the house, and the others decided to keep it a secret. Jack told us he needed to go to the next town on an errand. When he returned we felt such joy when Mother Hayden stepped out of the station wagon! Thus, we were married with church friends and many of our family members in attendance.

The wedding was scheduled for the afternoon, but it ended up happening much later than we had originally planned. The groomsmen and boys that were participating were staying at a friend's house four miles from the church. They were driving back and forth in Dick's station wagon. Unfortunately, when they were dressed and ready to go to the church, they could not find the keys to the car. There was no phone at the church, so they couldn't tell anyone what had happened or ask where the keys might be. (This was long before cell phones.) Dick had tossed the keys on a bed, and in the excitement, the boys had thrown their clothes on top of the bed over the keys. Finally, someone found them and they raced off to the church. Though our ceremony was a bit late, we were just as married.

Although a little late, we were just as married.

Early the next morning, the trusty blue and white station wagon was loaded and the newly-weds and their wedding party prepared to go. How we hated to tell his mother goodbye after such a short time, but we had to get everyone back to college. The group was missing classes to come to our wedding. That non-stop drive back to Walla Walla was hilarious. The young people had decorated the wagon to fit the occasion, so at every stop for gas, we were the subject of interesting discussions. People must have scratched their heads when they saw six people in the honeymoon car rather than two!

One of our first priorities after marriage was to contact the GC to give them official notice that we were available for overseas mission service. We realized that an opening might not be immediately available, so we tucked the idea in the back of our minds until they decided to contact us.

Since Dick had a job in Tacoma, we settled there for a time, and I found work at the county hospital. The large wards were a new experience for me. Working with a nursing staff who liked to talk about who had thrown the largest objects at their husbands when they were angry was new to me. How we enjoyed Mt. Rainier in the fall and sightseeing other beautiful spots in the Tacoma area.

At this time Shirley and Herb and three pre-schoolers were living in Bakersfield, California near Bakersfield Junior Academy where Herb was teaching. A new gymnasium, which would double as a church, was being built. Shirley arranged for us to move to Bakersfield where Dick would work on the gym, and I could do clinic nursing. This sounded good to us, so off we went to Bakersfield, which made this the first of our many moves. My job in the clinic was a new and interesting experience. With his industrial arts background, Dick thoroughly enjoyed the building work. In the spring of that year, he was invited to teach the eighth grade starting the next fall. He accepted, but only for one year because he had decided he should return to school and earn a master's degree. By now, it was delightfully evident that the Hayden family would be three instead of two.

One sad day, a phone call came with word that Stella, my oldest sister in Fruita, Colorado, was seriously ill. Her youngest of four children was still breast-feeding when she began to have severe back problems. It became difficult for Stella to walk and to carry out her nursing duties. An x-ray of her back showed air pockets in her scapula and vertebra. A few weeks later, we realized she had aggressive breast cancer.

All our family met in Colorado for a last reunion together, but it was heart-wrenching. Mom stayed in Colorado for a time to care for her, but after while Mom needed to get home. Eventually she, Stella, and the four children traveled by train back to Iowa. When the crops were harvested, her husband would join them.

It seems when God permits sorrow, He always softens it with some token of joy. On June 17 our first child arrived, a lovely, perfect son. We hadn't thought to have a child so soon, but the timing of his birth was divine. We named him "Richard," like his father and grandfather, with each "Richard" having different middle names. He became "Richard Christian Hayden." We called him "Richie," as Dick had been called when he was little. Dick took one look at this beautiful baby boy and said, "He looks like me!" Indeed, he did, but his freckles would take a while to show.

The day he was born, I went to work at the clinic as usual. Knowing the delivery date wasn't far away, my doctor—and boss—examined me and declared, "You're not going to work today; you're going to the hospital!" When I held our baby in my arms, I felt a joy nothing could replace. Dick and I sensed the responsibility involved and wondered, 'How does one raise a child to love the Lord and to develop his own set of talents?'

Thankfully, having a baby did not change our activities. Richie went to the beach with us, on camping trips in the mountains, and on every other family outing. We had a baby carrier that usually went on Dick's back when we hiked.

Meanwhile, one day Mom phoned from Ruthven reporting that Stella could not get up. She asked if I would come help care for her. I flew home with my newborn. Counting baby Richie, there were five little ones in the house. Stella's oldest child was in the first grade, the youngest was only a year old. Who would assume responsibility for the children when their mother was so sick? She could still talk to them, but they needed more mothering than she could muster. Dad's relatives who lived in the area were very supportive. As Stella's condition worsened, they took the children home with them.

How could we continue without our oldest sister?

I cannot express the heartache I felt watching a loved-one's body deteriorate. Stella believed until her last breath that she would be healed. Many prayers ascended on her behalf. How could we let her go? She was needed so much. Her children needed their mother desperately. Her husband could hardly cope without his wife. She had been active, not only as a nurse, but also in the Sabbath School children's departments. Sadly, the physical healing we had all hoped for did not happen. The day came when we laid her to rest to await Jesus' return. The heartache was overwhelming. Caring for her was emotionally the most difficult thing I had ever done.

Even with that great sorrow, there was no loud weeping and wailing. We cried; yes, we cried hard, and our hearts bled, but we sorrowed quietly. How does one adjust to life without a loved one? I had often sought her advice, and that was no longer possible. I found that the early unwanted education in the way my culture handled sorrow was helpful. My nursing experience was also useful. Somehow life goes on. We had the hope of the soon-coming Savior and of the resurrection morning; never had we so longed for that day! I also had baby Richie to comfort me. He felt so good. Though God had allowed horrific pain, God had not abandoned me. I could see His footprints in the shadows. Unfortunately, two more shadows loomed just ahead.

As you may have detected by now, in Mom's and Dad's family, emotional displays were rare. Discussing one's feelings was seldom done. Was this a result of the harshness of pioneer life? Was it from the need to accept life as it was? Or was this a part of their European culture? Perhaps it was, in part, from the pain Mom carried after being shot in the leg? Seldom did she complain. It seemed one was expected to "grin and bear difficulties," and live above physical or emotional pain. I do not know why my family did not talk of their emotions, but that is the way it was. So, we continued on with pain in our hearts while carrying on with routine tasks.

Dick had been accepted as a master's student at Potomac University in Takoma Park, Maryland. When school was out at Bakersfield, we moved once more in that little station wagon, going first to Jack's graduation from Walla Walla College, then driving through the beautiful mountains and across the green fields of the plains to Iowa, stopping for a brief stop to visit my parents. The drive on to Washington, D.C. was my first trip east, so all of the scenery was extremely interesting to me. The plains of Iowa changed to the bluffs along the Mississippi, then to the flat-lands of Ohio. How different the mountains in the east were from those in the west—equally beautiful, but different. There were no freeways to speed us along to our destination, but at last the three of us arrived and settled into a seminary apartment.

I worked nights at Washington Adventist Hospital while Dick was the baby sitter. His days were spent going to classes and studying while I babysat.

One day soon after we had settled in to our new routine, a letter came that had been addressed by my father. This was the first letter ever I had received in his handwriting because Mom always did the writing. Something must be wrong! Indeed, something was terribly wrong. My youngest brother, Ivan, had graduated from Oak Park Academy in Nevada, Iowa that year and had stayed to work on the academy farm for the summer. He and a friend had motorcycles and had gone for an evening ride. As Ivan crossed railroad tracks, his motorcycle somehow hit the railroad tracks wrong, and catapulted him into the air. He landed with his face on the handle bars. Fortunately, the farm manager heard the scream and came running. His knowledge of first aid saved Ivan's life until the ambulance arrived and could take him to the nearest hospital. The doctors took one look at him, started an IV, and sent him on to a larger hospital in Des Moines. By the time my parents were notified, Ivan was already in surgery at the hospital in Des Moines, 200 miles away. Mom and Dad hurried

Ivan, the youngest in the family graduates from the academy.

to the hospital in time to meet the surgeons as they were coming out from surgery. "We've done the best we can for the young man, but we don't expect he will survive."

Kind friends in Des Moines offered them a place to stay. Dad had farm work that needed to be done, so after a few days, he drove back home, leaving Mom by Ivan's bedside. In this tragedy, I yearned to go and help, but that was not possible, as I needed to work to support the family while Dick went to school. I was so thankful for family friends who took on the role I felt I should have filled. Rozella, who we now called "Rosy," lived in Nevada and visited as often as she could.

Mom stayed with Ivan for weeks as he gradually regained consciousness. The plastic surgeon would stand by his bedside and look at his work for a long time. Mom asked him why he gazed at him. The surgeon replied, "I rarely have the privilege of seeing my work after this type of surgery, as most patients with this much injury do not live." He added, "If he does live, and if he is able to see again, he will see double if the cheek bones are not the exactly the same height." After regaining consciousness, Ivan did not know many things. Mom taught him to eat again, as well as care for many of his other needs that the busy staff did not have time to do.

His eyesight was not the greatest concern. More problematic was his brain. The brain specialist doubted he would recover mentally, but he gave no prognosis. At the time Mom was president of the Association for Retarded Children. She knew a little about what brain injuries can mean to the person and to their family. As Ivan improved, he remembered his earlier life, but could not remember recent happenings. Finally, the day arrived when Dad came down to get them. Ivan could go home.

During the following months as Mom cared for Ivan at home, another situation brought sorrow to all of us. Rosy went through a difficult divorce. After separating, her husband tried to kidnap their two boys and make life very miserable for her. Our hearts ached for her as she struggled with the divorce and with concerns about her future. Sometimes I wondered, 'Which difficulty was harder: a health struggle or a divorce?'

After about three months of caring for Ivan at home, Mom took him back to Des Moines for a follow-up doctor visit. It was apparent the plastic surgeon had done an excellent repair. Not only could Ivan see, but he saw normally with the same glasses prescription he had used before the accident! But he remembered nothing of the accident or of having been in the hospital. On the way home, they stopped to see Ivan's motor cycle. Miles later, Mom stopped to get gas and Ivan went into the bathroom. He stayed so long that Mom began to worry that something had happened to him. Finally he came out. After looking around a bit, he asked, "What are we doing here?"

Mom explained, "I just took you to see your doctors, and now we are returning home."

"Why did we need to see the doctors?" He asked.

"Ivan, you had a terrible motorcycle accident," she replied. He did not remember having just seen his wrecked motorcycle. Though he could not remember the accident or recall being at the hospital, from that day on, he was normal. It was not long before he wanted to go to work, and then head on to college.

All of these difficulties brought up questions in the family. Why? Why was Stella, who believed she would be healed, who was an active participant in praying for healing, and who seemed so urgently needed, not healed? Why was Ivan, who was unconscious, and knew nothing of the many prayers ascending in his behalf, healed (though he was not healed immediately)? Why didn't God heal them both? Why? Why? Why? Perhaps God knew that to lose their oldest and youngest children in one year, in addition to having a divorce in the family, would be too much for Mom and Dad? Perhaps God would use Ivan's healing for the redemption of some soul? Of one thing we were certain, only God knew the real answer. With Ivan's healing, we also realized anew that God was able to heal, and it gave us evidence that God cared about us and was interested in our lives. We were most thankful we had Ivan, and we begged God to help us trust where things didn't make sense.

Back in Takoma Park, our life hurried on. There was an opening at Columbia Union College for a nursing arts classroom instructor. (Nursing arts is the beginning nursing course.) Alice Smith, dean of the nursing school, asked me to accept that position, so I changed jobs. I enjoyed teaching those lively beginning nursing students, and it was a relief to no longer work nights, but the change necessitated finding a babysitter.

One day in staff meeting, Alice mentioned her need for a secretary. I thought of Rosy's situation, and suggested her name to Alice. The position worked out for both of them, and soon Rosy was settled in Takoma Park. What delight she and the boys added to our lives! Since Washington, D.C. is adjacent to Takoma Park, we decided to dedicate Fridays to visiting important government places and historical sites. By the end of the year, we still had so many left to see. Even so, it was a special time to get acquainted with our government and history. On occasional weekends, we took time to go to various nearby battlefields. Richie and I joined Dick's class on a New England Adventist history tour, a trip I highly recommend!

At long last, Dick's classes were finished, and he was awarded his master's in education. The wives of graduating students were unofficially given "PHT's" (Putting Hubby Through). Once again, graduation meant saying goodbye to friends. This time we had to leave Rosy and her boys as well. We packed up and were soon on our way to Sandia View Academy in New Mexico where Dick would be boys' dean, and I would be school nurse and teach biology.

Rosy, Greg and Doug enlivened our lives.

Chapter 7

Pastures Green; Waters Still

Our year at Sandia View Academy in Albuquerque, New Mexico, was a hard year for the school. It was the first year for the principal to occupy that position, the first year for Dick to be dean of boys, and the first year for a missionary from Lebanon to be dean of girls. It seemed we spent most of our time in discipline committee. At the end of the year, the dean of girls moved on, and since an opportunity opened for us, so did we. With this move, our lives brightened.

Dick had been asked to be principal and teach the upper grades in Salinas, California. Salinas treated us to wonderful camping areas, places to hike, and access to Monterrey Bay with its seal-watching and tide-pools. By now, Richie was a good hiker.

I worked nights two days a week in labor and delivery at Salinas Community Hospital until another pregnancy made it difficult to work. There was something about labor and delivery that was contagious, for on May 28, 1962 after only a two-hour labor, Carmen Estelle was born. The baby carrier came into use once again.

How Carmen enriched our family! She was a good and beautiful baby with brownish hair and light brown eyes. Everyone said she looked like me. We laughed when one of our visiting friends commented that she already

Dad gives his son instructions on riding.

had her eyes open.

Richie, nearly four-years-old now, had been excited over getting a new sister or brother, but was disappointed because his little sister could not play with him—all she did was eat and sleep.

In the summer Dick worked at Wawona, a junior camp inside of the boundaries of Yosemite. Richie was delighted when Dick took him horse-back riding. (Dick took Carmen, too, but she wasn't quite as impressed.) Grandpa and Grandma Hayden spent one summer at camp with us. The camp director honored Grandpa with a special badge that said, "Top-notch Grandpa babysitter."

We enjoyed our time at Salinas. The two years we spent there were good to us. However, the enrollment was declining, and the board was forced to downgrade to a one-teacher school. The lower-grade teacher took over, and we moved on to Burlingame, California where Dick took a similar position.

Burlingame was in the city, a big adjustment for us, but it was not without its own joys. Living near San Francisco, we had the pleasure of taking visitors to see the sights. Here Dick's love for music found new opportunities. He often led song service at church, sang solos, and played his trumpet. In Burlingame, he couldn't find enough other singers to form a quartet, but he did find someone with whom he could sing duets. They often sang for church. They made quite a pair since the other man was well over six feet tall and portly, and Dick was five-foot-eight and lean.

Still struggling with the idea of finding some way to put together a quartet, Dick thought of his friend, Mario Ruf, who taught at Mountain View Academy which was not far from us. The two men recorded two parts and then played the recording while they sang the other two parts. Mario sang the higher tenor parts, Dick the baritone and bass. They found that two good men could sing four good parts quite fine.

In the spring of that year, Dick agreed to teach another year for Burlingame. We thought we were going to settle there for a time, but it was not to be. Dick soon received an invitation to Armona Union Academy to teach history, Bible, and Spanish, as well as drive the bus. The educational superintendent encouraged him to take this job, as it was considered a promotion. So, we packed again and left the friends we had made there.

That first year at Armona we lived in an old farm house near Cutler. It was surrounded by grape vineyards, olive and orange groves, as well as fields of cucumbers. I dried many grapes, so raisins were an important part of our diet that year. The children enjoyed our rabbit and two cats. Much to their delight, one cat had kittens. The rabbit lived outdoors with the cats. Whenever we came outside, he hopped to us to be petted and fed.

On Friday evenings we opened Sabbath with a candlelight supper of fruit soup or salad and cinnamon rolls. We usually invited company to come to our home after church on Sabbath, then we all took walks or went interesting places together.

That year Dick's sister, Carolyn, married Burton. Richie was the Bible boy, and Carmen was the flower girl. Both looked and acted like angels, but unfortunately, Carmen fell into the pool after the ceremony. She still looked like an angel but a very wet one.

The next joyful event of the year was the arrival of Rodney Grant on September 6, 1964. He was born on a Sunday, making it easy for Dick to care for Richie and Carmen while I was at the hospital. Rodney had reddish-blond hair with yellow-green eyes. From the day he was born, his eyes sparkled with mischief.

How special to be Bible boy and flower girl for Carolyn's wedding.

What a blessing the three happy healthy children were! As a family with young children we camped, hiked, and yes, even backpacked. Wherever we went, the children went. Dick got a kick out of teaching the children to "tumble" even before they could walk; the kids always begged for more. When Richie started first grade, our lives centered the children's education. I was a full-time mother, a role I found to be more satisfying than any other career I ever had. I saw mothering as a God-given privilege. My sole purpose was to help my children develop into the people God would have them be and to be a companion to my husband. Those years with my children and husband were the best of my life.

The principal of Armona decided his bus driver needed to live in the Armona/Hanford area rather than the Cutler area. It seemed apparent that rather than serve the Lord in some distant land, the Lord's plan for us was to work in the United States, so we decided to put down roots.

Backpacking in Yosemite

We purchased our first home in the country near Armona. It was a lovely brick home on an acre-plus, complete with irrigation ditches. Some of the land was in pasture, the remainder in orchard—peach, almond, walnut trees, and more. We "settled in" with a pony and a calf, bicycles and a tricycle. How we enjoyed living near Sequoia and Kings Canyon National Parks.

Needing some additional income to make house payments, I began working part-time at the Hanford Community Hospital. It had once been a community hospital, but the Seventh-day Adventists had purchased and rebuilt it. It was a comfortable place to work.

What fun to ride. Rodney isn't so sure.

Dick's parents had gone to Peru as missionaries soon after they were married. Now they were almost ready to retire. Dick and his brother, Jack, decided to visit them one more time and tour Peru. This was home to Dick and Jack, and they both eagerly looked forward to the trip. They plotted the journey so it would also count toward some educational credits they each needed. Dick had been taking classes at Pacific Union College the previous summer, and he had planned a history project on the architecture of the beautiful buildings in Peru. Jack was earning his master's in special education. He and his professor planned a study of special education for them to do while they were in Peru.

But this was a year of surprises. My sister, Shirley, called and informed me that Mom and Dad had been in a car accident. They left that morning from her Pennsylvania home headed for Boston to visit Mom's brother, Richard, but they never arrived in Boston. On a four-lane highway, a driver on the inside lane made a right-hand turn in front of them. The resulting accident left Dad with a fractured patella (knee), and Mom with a femur (leg) fractured both horizontally and vertically, as well as a fractured ankle. They were hospitalized in New York. Mom was put in traction with the prognosis that she would never walk again, but the doctors didn't know my mother's determination. After the traction was removed, she was moved to Reading Rehabilitation Center in Pennsylvania where Shirley could visit her. Contrary to predictions, Mom went home walking in a brace. She commented that the process was so painful that she hoped that if she were ever in another accident, it would kill her. I was sorry my responsibilities kept me from going to be with her. Instead, I sent her something every day she was hospitalized.

Maybe standing on a tricycle was a little safer.

In the midst of all this, Dick arrived home one day and asked me sit down and read a letter with him. The letter was from the GC secretariat asking us to go to Mayaguez, Puerto Rico where Dick would be principal and teach the upper grades in the school established for missionary children. Bella Vista Hospital is a Seventh-day Adventist hospital located on the hill above Mayaguez. A number of English-speaking missionary families were stationed there, and their children needed an English-speaking school to attend. One never knows what to expect in life!

Would we go? Would we sell our dream house on the farm? What if the house didn't sell? Would we take our children to another country to live? Were we willing to down-size to make another move? Would we still be able to visit Peru?

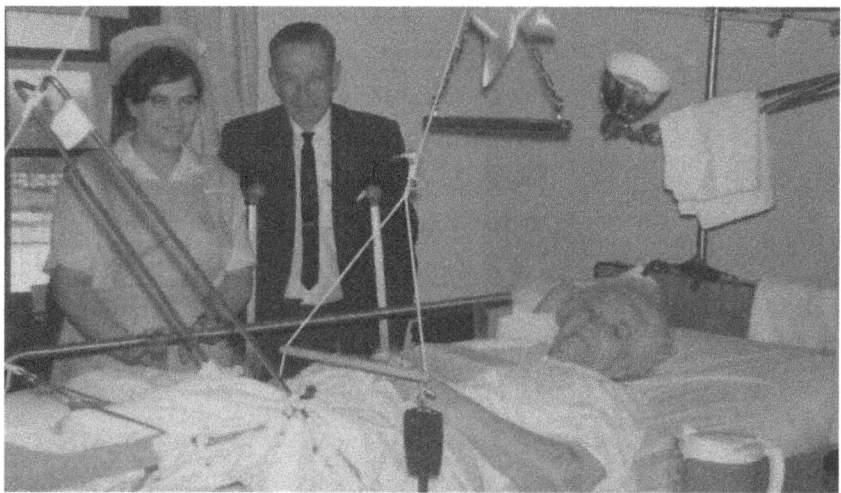

Life takes unexpected turns.

Chapter 8

In Righteous Paths, Puerto Rico

Yes, we had committed ourselves to mission service when we were first married. Of course we would go to Puerto Rico!

When the call came, we were consumed with preparations for our trip to Peru. We wondered, 'Do we cancel our plans, or can we still make that trip?' The GC agreed we could go. They would pay our salary, and we would handle the travel expenses.

Besides preparing for the Peru tour, we started caring for a myriad of other items that demand attention in getting ready for this type of move—sorting, packing, and trying to sell our home. The most distasteful to the children were the immunizations. Richie and Rodney both fainted at the sight of the needles.

We needed to get our car from the west coast to the port in Miami, so it could be shipped on to Puerto Rico. We made a quick trip across the United States by way of Iowa to see my parents. Mom had arrived home shortly before we arrived. She was walking but with some pain. Our children were fascinated with Grandma's brace. Dad's knee had healed, but he was unable to farm all his land, so he had ended up leasing out part of it. Dad's physical injuries seemed minor compared to his emotional trauma. He felt the accident was his fault, and he seemed unable to find a way to forgive himself. In actuality it was the other driver's fault. We were plenty thankful they had survived!

Sliding in the sand dunes gave a welcome break from riding in the crowded car.

The trip to Peru was fantastic. Grandma and Grandpa Hayden met us in Lima and took us in their VW (Volkswagen) bug (not a VW bus) up north to Chiclayo. Grandma and Grandpa had agreed to care for our children while we toured Peru. Carmen and Rodney stayed in Chiclayo with Grandpa and Grandma Hayden. Richie was given the option of staying with them or going with us. It was explained to him than on such a trip one cannot always get a drink when desired, nor use the toilet, etc. He chose to go with us.

We were quite a traveling group. There were the three of us, plus Jack, his wife, and his instructor; that made six. For part of the trip, two student missionaries joined us.

The trip to Iquitos was very special to Dick and Jack. The mission station in Iquitos was still similar to how Dick remembered it. It was where he was born and had grown up, with the exception of a few years in the highlands. (Midwife Anna Stahl delivered him there, bringing him through a difficult breach delivery. The story of his birth is recorded in the book by R.A. Hayden, *From Football Field to Mission Field*, which was published in 1951.) Huge, beautiful trees grew in front of the homes, the church, and hospital. Across the road was the ever-changing Amazon River. The missionaries welcomed us royally, took us on tours, and arranged for a trip on the Amazon in the Auxiliadora, the very boat Grandpa Hayden had brought up from Brazil and had used so many years on the Amazon.

Some other highlights of the trip included visiting Nevati, a jungle mission station with a clinic, thatched-roof church, school, and an air strip. The mission's only contact with the outside world was via radio. We happened to arrive the weekend of camp meeting and were able to witness a large baptism with four pastors baptizing simultaneously in the river. The highlands were just as interesting, but quite a contrast to the jungle with their treeless mountains, cool temperatures, high altitudes, and Lake Titicaca. There was no heat in the homes, even though the water on the street froze at nights. Cuzco took us back in

In Righteous Paths, Puerto Rico

A last picture in Chiclayo of the Hayden family. Carolyn and her family had been there a year earlier.

history hundreds of years. After a memorable trip, we went to Lima for quick visits to historical places and buildings and then inched our way back up the coast for a final weekend in Chiclayo. For this girl from the plains of Iowa, the trip was a fascinating, eye-opening introduction to mission life and to the wonders of the world.

Our goodbyes were said too soon, and it wasn't long before our family was boarding a plane for Puerto Rico.

Arriving at the hospital in Mayaguez, we were pleasantly surprised to find our belongings already in the house assigned to us. The beds were unpacked and made ready for us to rest from our travels. We found Puerto Rico to be a beautiful island and soon fell in love with the people, the missionaries, the beaches, the "mountain trails," as well as our work. While Dick taught the children, I worked at the hospital and taught in the nursing school associated with Antillian Union College across the valley.

Dick's knowledge of Spanish was most useful, as some of his students were from the community and had no knowledge of English when they started school. They soon learned English, but they initially needed some coaching in Spanish.

The poinsettias in Puerto Rico were large bushes.

He also translated for church services and other meetings. The language was a real challenge for me, especially when I was trying to teach nursing students. The first-year students took their classes at the college in Spanish with Spanish textbooks. The next year they transferred to the hospital for their clinical subjects. There English was used, and the textbooks were in English. When the students started, many understood no verbal English. One student, though, came from the English-speaking St. Thomas Island and understood no Spanish when she came to the college to study nursing. The first few weeks were difficult, but she quickly learned Spanish and became a straight-A student. Believe me, we all learned together! In working with the students, I discovered that Puerto Ricans were very open with their feelings. When tragedy struck, they wept hysterically. Perhaps this openness was one reason why they were such a loving and lovable people.

Our home was simple. Being in the tropics, it had louvered windows. The floors were tile. In the back yard, there was a stand of banana trees. In the front yard, there was a Corazon tree, a huge avocado tree, and a breadfruit tree. Corazon is a tree with soft, sweet sop fruit. It's delicious. There are a number of different kinds of sweet and sour sop tropical fruit. The sweet sop (we think) is the fruit of heaven! Sour sop was used mainly for a delicious drink. "Corazon" means "heart," referring to the shape of the fruit. The breadfruit dropped on the road below and made a mess. The avocados were so large that three of them would fill a shoebox. That is where I learned to like avocados. The bottom of the front door did not fit the sill quite right, so there was space for the cockroaches to enter the house at will. Cockroaches were one of the unpleasant realities of the tropics along with mold on shoes and books. But if you loved nature, it was a paradise of beautiful flowers, birds, interesting sea shells, snakes, lizards, frogs, and bugs.

We had a lot of adventures while we were in Puerto Rico. The hospital owned a beach house, so we picnicked there from time to time. Some of the missionaries had cabins in the Mangrove Islands located on the south side of the island. They invited us to go boating with them there some weekends. We also found time to go see Phosphorescent Bay, where the water sparkles and glows at night.

We had heard that Puerto Ricans do not swim in the months starting with "J." I learned why one day when I was water skiing. The skis flipped me into the water, and I landed in a multitude of jellyfish. There were jellyfish everywhere I put an arm or leg. Yeah, eventually the skis and I made it back into the boat, but I stung all day, like I had been bathing in nettles.

Beautiful Puerto Rico

We loved Puerto Rico, but after only a year, life took another unexpected turn when Dick was asked to go to Nicaragua to be the director of the departments for the mission (with the exception of the education department). This time Dick built a container so we could ship our things to Managua, Nicaragua. Our car was sent on a boat headed to Miami. It seemed like God was always keeping us on the move.

Chapter 9
New Righteous Paths, Nicaragua

We flew to Miami, arriving in time to enjoy the fun of watching our car being unloaded from the ship. Then the adventure began as we traveled overland to Nicaragua. From Miami, we drove to the Everglades, then to Alabama, Mississippi, and Louisiana. Texas was next with a stop at the home of my brother, Lyle. I was happy that my children were able to meet cousins they had never before seen. After that, we headed for the Mexican border.

Dick had dreamed for years of making this trip, and it was all he anticipated. Montemorelos, now a university, was one of our first stops. Dick had read many stories about the "flying doctor" of Montemorelos, so he wanted to see the airstrip. Times had changed. That doctor was no longer at the hospital. An accident had caused the airstrip to be closed. Piles of gravel had been dumped on it to keep anyone from landing.

We stopped beside the road to eat. Rodney is holding his bowl to show that he ate it all.

A truck had pulled us out.

From poor country roads to the congested streets of Mexico City, we felt God's protection. There were no warnings of stopped vehicles or about livestock in the road. In southern Mexico on a stretch of road under construction, we got stuck in the mud and had to be pulled out. The roads did get better. Eventually, we arrived in Guatemala City and the office of the Central American Union in Guatemala and were welcomed to the Central American Union, which is a part of the Inter-American Division, an administrative unit of the Seventh-day Adventist Church. We kept going on through El Salvador where we stopped to see the Fords (of *These Fords still Run* by Barbara Westphal). It was a privilege to meet this fascinating couple who had dedicated their lives to serving God in Central America. They had chosen to remain living in El Salvador after retirement because their hearts were anchored there; besides, what would he do in the United States once he got to the place he could not drive? He didn't need a car in El Salvador because buses took him everywhere he wanted to go.

Central American Union Office.

After navigating borders in Mexico, Guatemala, El Salvador, and Honduras, the all-important border crossing finally arrived—the one entering Nicaragua. The first stop was at Hospital Adventista de Nicaragua in northern Nicaragua. This was a busy hospital serving patients not only from northern Nicaragua but from as far as Managua as well. The last stretch was a 70-mile drive to Managua, our final destination.

Hospital Adventista de Nicaragua.

In Managua, we were welcomed by the mission president, son of the pioneer Fords in El Salvador. He was packing to return to the United States on furlough. We rented their home on a hill outside of Managua which had a large fenced yard where the children could play. Ford's dog came with the deal. It had belonged to the people who had rented before him and was believed to keep away thieves.

Dick was soon busy with his work at the mission, and I kept occupied teaching our children—with the help of Home Study Institute. Richie was now in the third grade, and Carmen was in the first.

One item that had to be cared for quickly was to register our car. We had a VW squareback Rabbit, just large enough to carry our family. Then came the shocker. When Dick went to register it, he learned that the duty on a car was the price of a new car. Just a few days before, the government had enacted a law stating that all imported cars must pay 100% duty. What should we do? We certainly did not have the money to pay that price. We discovered that a missionary from another denomination wished to sell his good-sized van. Dick agreed to purchase it, and a student missionary happily drove our VW up to Auburn, California for Dick's brother to sell for us. The Lord knew that our VW was not adequate for the needs of our family and of the mission. The van was usually loaded with people and/or things everywhere we went.

Our next challenge was clearing our shipment through customs. What a pain customs officials can be. However, once we navigated that hurdle, it was nice to surround ourselves with familiar things.

Managua was almost at sea level, and it was hot! Our home was at a higher elevation and a bit cooler. We joked that if the termites stopped holding hands, the house would fall down. The house was arranged a strange way. The bathroom was larger than many bedrooms. We put the washer and drier in the bathroom. The shower was big enough for all of us to shower at one time, but we never tried it. Hot water had to be heated on the stove. We learned to shower early in the evening when it still felt good to take a cool shower. Oh yes, we also had a toad that decided to inhabit our shower. The toads in the tropics are the size of a small dog. It never bothered anyone, and we were happy for it to come out into the hallway at night and eat bugs. (The outside wall of the hallway was a chain-link fence.)

There were fruit trees—mangos, a mamey (I haven't seen one anywhere else), many cashews, papaya, and guava. The cashew fruit smelled so bad that we didn't bring it into the kitchen until we were ready to use it, but it made a good drink.

Birds were numerous. One tree I called the "oriole tree," because so many orioles roosted there. An unexpected bonus was a pair of motmots that had found our bank to their liking and nested there. Motmots are colorful birds whose tails look like small tennis rackets.

In Puerto Rico our children had played mostly with other missionary children, so they did not learn much Spanish. But being the only missionaries in Managua, it didn't take long until all three were chattering away in Spanish. All three of them were learning new things every day. One of Carmen's Home Study lessons asked her, "Do you know any children who are different from you?" That week she had played with her Spanish friends and with three black children, but she had not played with any white friends. She responded to the question, "No." Poor little Rodney hated going to the supermarket in Managua because the women couldn't keep their hands off his soft blond hair.

Richie decided he wanted a gila monster. He caught one in a rock pile where the cactus grew. One day, it got out of the cage. He called for help. We all went running to see what we could do. That big lizard jumped and ran like lightning. We finally managed to chase it out the door, down the stairs, and outside. We never saw it near the house again.

The children love to participate in any activity Daddy was doing.

A memorable experience was a trip on Lake Nicaragua to Omotepe Island. The Adventists on the island had not been visited for a very long time. We pulled the mission boat to the lake and loaded it with provisions for the weekend. It was a beautiful drive on a Friday afternoon over the curvy mountainous roads. Quickly launching the boat, for it would soon be Sabbath, we headed for the town where the church was located. Dick was able to find the church elder. He let us into the church to stay for the night. The church benches were our beds, and we had water which came from a spigot in the courtyard. On Sabbath, we worshiped with the few people who came to church, then set out on foot to visit others in their homes. Our hearts were saddened as they bemoaned that no pastor had called on them for years, even for family funerals. We wished we could arrange for someone to come more often, but none was available, and we were unable.

On Sunday, we hiked many miles trying to find members. It was warm, and we did not have enough water with us. The hospitable people in one home offered us coconut milk to drink. One of them climbed the coconut tree and cut off a green coconut for each of us, hacked the tops off, and offered it to us to drink. How good it tasted. It was late afternoon by the time we were back in the boat, and later still when we arrived at our vehicle. Sunset at that latitude is at about 6:00 p.m. much of the year, so we drove home in the dark. On a curvy stretch, Dick followed a very slow-moving truck for some distance. Finally, not seeing headlights from any approaching vehicle, he pulled around to pass. He was at the point of no return, when his headlights brought to view a large ox in the middle of our lane. Dick stepped on the brakes, and the boat trailer started to fishtail. That was not an option! We knew we were headed for disaster. When we thought there would be a crash, the ox suddenly disappeared, and we went on our way thanking the Lord for His protection.

When Dick traveled to the various churches, he would take us with him as much as possible. One of the most interesting and inspiring visits we made was to an area in the mountains above Matagalpa to the home of Secundino. As a farmer, Secundino raised a variety of crops and took the produce by bus into Managua to sell. One day in Managua, he met a relative who asked him if he would like to have a Bible. Secundino happily accepted. Back home, he tried to read it, but his schooling had been so limited, he really could not it. The next time he went to Managua, he saw his relative again. When questioned about the Bible, Secundino admitted that he had tried to read it, but he didn't know how. His relative then offered him some Voice of Prophecy Bible Lessons.

Dick loved the adventure of traveling to the mountain villages. Sometimes he forded rivers.

Back home, Secundino persisted in studying the lessons and the Bible. It took about a month to study each lesson, but as he continued, to his delight, he found he could read better and better. He gave his heart to the Lord and taught his family to love the message he had learned. Now his heart burned with the desire to share what he had found. Farming had required that he spend his days protecting the crops from parrots and other creatures that wanted to get the harvest before he did. How could he go and share his love for Jesus? He promised God that if God would protect his crops, he would ride over the mountains on his horse and share the wonderful news of Jesus' love and soon return. God prospered him both in his farming and in winning others to Jesus. In time, he came to the mission to ask for a pastor to come and baptize his converts. The group grew big enough to form a small congregation. They worshiped outside, but it was apparent they needed a chapel. What could be done? For the moment we could only pray that God would provide. He answered that prayer in a totally unexpected way.

A special time in Nicaragua was when my parents visited us. Dick planned a special itinerary to show them the country, our work, and to have Mother Hansen help tell stories to the children. Included in the plan was a trip to Bluefields and Corn Island to present Sabbath School workshops. Eastern Nicaragua speaks English, so language was no problem there. We loaded the boat on our trailer and drove to the Escondido River. There we launched it, loaded our supplies, and headed downstream. There was not enough room for all of us in the small boat, so Dick and Dad Hansen went down in the mission boat, while the rest of us took the commercial ship. Mom was fascinated with the culture she observed—the lice crawling in the people's hair, and the little girls always caring for the younger children rather than the mothers.

Finally a village was reached, visits made and a meeting held.

Once we arrived in Bluefields, Mom was shocked to discover that Pastor Houghton was a black man. It had not occurred to her that we would be staying in the home of a black family. She quickly overcame her surprise and enjoyed the family as much as we did. She couldn't keep from touching the fuzzy hair of their little girl, just like the women in Managua had touched Rodney's soft, blond hair. Being about the same age, our children were happy as a pack of puppies playing with the three Houghton children. Completing the meetings in Bluefields, it was time to fly to Corn Island.

Corn Island is very warm, and the people are friendly. We stayed in the home of some people who had a turkey. Every time the children wanted to go outside, the turkey took after them. The owners ended up putting a metal basket over him so he wouldn't peck them. Mom and Dad were able to wade out in the water far enough to enjoy the beautiful tropical fish.

The economy of Corn Island is based on coconuts. When the coconut is ripe, they cut off the green husk and then put the brown hard shell on a hollowed-out pole about knee high. Then with their machetes, they chip off the shells, and dry the coconuts. The coconuts are then shipped out of the country to processing plants. Copra, dried coconut, is used in many products.

Our seminar for children's Sabbath School was well accepted. The audiences were delighted with Mom's stories. Mom moved about amazingly well with her newly-healed leg, but she wasn't always able to walk as far as she would have liked.

Eventually, the needs of the Nicaraguan mission changed, and we were sent to live at the hospital where Dick became Bible teacher and chaplain, as well as pastor of the northern part of Nicaragua. He continued as youth director for the mission. Again, I taught in the nursing school. The elementary school on the hospital campus was in Spanish. Since our children could already speak Spanish, this gave them an opportunity to learn to read it as well. Richie and Carmen attended the school while I supplemented their learning with some classes from Home Study Institute.

The hospital compound was arranged in the form of a large square with the hospital in the front near the road. The houses were down the sides, and the nursing school with the dormitory was in the back. In the center was a large grassy area where the children on campus played. When it was time to call my kids home, I used a police whistle.

All of the missionaries at the hospital were very busy, and this is what sparked the discussion described in the introduction to this book. With so much to do, how would the Lord have us set our priorities? Just how does He lead His children? How was He leading me?

Looking back, I could see how God had blessed me. I had a Godly husband and beautiful, noble children. I was fulfilling the dreams of my childhood by doing front-line mission work. God had protected our family and placed us where we could make a significant contribution. What more could my heart desire?

Chapter 10

Yea, Though I Cry

Three years in the Inter-American Division passed quickly, and soon it was time for furlough. As we were planning our itinerary, a Peace Corps couple in La Trinidad, the nearby village, asked Dick if he would consider picking up a VW bus for them in the States, then drive it back to Nicaragua. Dick agreed, which meant that we had the use of their VW van for our trip across the United States.

We flew into Miami and picked up the VW. At the airport all three children were totally amazed that everyone spoke English; sadly, this ended their use of Spanish.

Auburn, California, (just north and east of Sacramento) was our west coast destination. After their retirement to the United States, Dick's parents had chosen to settle in Auburn where Dick's brother, Jack, and his family lived. Dick planned our furlough in such a way that allowed him to take flying lessons so he could achieve his instrument rating.

Leaving Nicaragua.

My parents and a brother and sister with their children.

What a wonderful trip that was! We crossed the country visiting Dick's sister and brother-in-law, Carolyn and Burton, in Virginia, Rosy and her boys in Takoma Park, my parents in Ruthven, and we stayed with aunts, uncles, cousins, and friends along the way. As we passed from state to state, the children kept asking, "Where's the border crossing?" The boys loved watching Uncle Stemple milk the cows in his big barn in Hutchinson, Minnesota. We also managed to tuck in some sightseeing. We stopped by the Badlands, Mount Rushmore, Yellowstone National Park, and the American Falls in Idaho. Richie, Carmen, and Rodney especially liked the Black Hills, Badlands, and "Old Faithful" in Yellowstone. We rode sailboats, feasted on strawberries, camped outdoors, and even saw snow at our campsite at Sylvan Lake in Yellowstone. For three kids having just left the tropics, nothing pleased them more than making snowmen. We had so much fun; it almost seemed too good to be true.

Our trek took us by way of Angwin and Pacific Union College to visit Dick's academy and college friends. (Angwin is north of San Francisco.) Our work in Nicaragua was very clearly the topic of interest. Dick described our youth camp situated on a volcanic lake, which we could not access by road. Dick explained that we went as far as we could by land. From there, we had to launch the mission boat, load it with the necessary food and other gear for camp, and then boat over to the camp. He mentioned that the boat motor was old and difficult to keep running. Dick's friends listened eagerly to our tales. We loved our visit, but it was time to press on to our ultimate western location—Grandpa and Grandma Hayden and brother Jack and family in Auburn, CA. What a joyful time we all had together.

After some time had passed, one of his friends phoned us in Auburn with some amazing news—the Angwin pathfinder club had decided to donate a new motor for the mission boat. Our problem then was: how could we get the motor to us in time? We only had a few days before we were scheduled to begin our trip back to Nicaragua. We needed to leave Auburn in time to spend Sabbath in Denver with my sister, Grace, and her family.

Dick, having just been training for his pilot's instrument rating, decided he should rent the same Cessna 172 on which he had taken lessons and fly to Pacific Union College where he would stay overnight and return the next day. Meanwhile, I could pack the vehicle, and we would all be on our way to Denver when he returned. Richie and Rodney decided to go with him. Carmen and I did not enjoy flying, so we chose to stay in Auburn with Grandma and Grandpa Hayden. (Whenever I flew, I had a problem with motion sickness.) Grandpa took them to the airport that pleasant Tuesday in November. How happy the boys were to be able to go on this little adventure. As a crow flies, it was only about 80 miles from Auburn to Angwin.

To three children from the tropics, this was a real treat.

The next afternoon was rainy. As arranged, Grandpa Hayden went to the airport to collect Dick and the boys. About four o'clock, as I was standing by the large window in the living room looking out at the humming birds coming to Grandma's feeder, I felt something brush against my arm. How odd. Turning to see who it was, I saw no one. It was a strange happening with no logical explanation. I registered it in my thoughts.

Grandpa came back alone with catastrophic news: Dick and the boys had not arrived at the airport. It was soon confirmed that they had taken off from the airport near Pacific Union College. Where were they?

What an evening and night that was! I alternated between hoping they had landed somewhere with no means to contact us and fearing they had crashed. Without sleeping, I prayed and waited; waited and prayed.

The following morning the telephone rang, and the worst message came: The plane had tried to land in a field in Pope Valley, had crashed into trees, and had burned on impact. Dick, Richie, and Rodney were dead.

At the news, I wished I were Puerto Rican and could become hysterical, but I wasn't, and I didn't. The controlled expression of grief demonstrated by my grandparents, parents, and other relatives was still my heritage. Their example had trained me how to relate to life's sorrows and disappointments, so I sobbed quietly.

Further information about the accident detailed that they had experienced adverse weather conditions—low ceiling clouds, rain, and fog. The fog had obstructed the pilot's vision at the accident site, about five miles from Angwin.

Dick had been alerted of possible weather problems, but apparently feeling the pressure to keep schedule, took off in less-than-ideal conditions. Probably his newly-acquired instrument skills gave him extra courage to make the flight.

In that sickening moment when I comprehended the horrific news, I learned firsthand that in His leading, God does not always protect His beloved children from tragedy, heartache, and crying.

Amidst all the evil of that day, I also learned something else about God's love and care for me. When I found out the exact time the accident had happened, something clicked. That sad event was recorded as happening at four o'clock on Wednesday, November 4, 1970, at the very time when I had felt a brush against my arms. To this day I believe my angel touched me at the time of the accident to tell me that heaven understood; although God had allowed this experience, He would not leave me to face it alone. That brush with an angel's wing has comforted me ever since.

"Yea, though I walk through the valley of the shadow of death, I will fear no evil: for thou art with me." Ps. 23:4.

Enjoying the park with Grandpa and Grandma.

Chapter 11

Supported by God's Staff

Life as I had known it had ended. In fact, I felt my whole life had ended. How could I go on living when my heart was dead? The first difficult task that must be done was to notify my parents, brothers, and sisters, as well as Dick's sister. How could I tell them? Jack (Dick's brother) kindly took over and phoned my parents first. After he had told them, I talked with my mother who had answered the phone. After sobbing together, she said that she would phone the others.

That week is a blur. I would not have survived without the support of God's staff—family, friends, church members, neighbors, and my invisible heavenly family! Dick's sister and family came from Ft. Belvoir, Virginia. My parents arrived as well as all of my brothers and sisters with some of the spouses, along with many family friends. A kind neighbor invited as many as possible to stay in their home.

The Hayden extended family and friends came for mutual support.

Many decisions had to be made, decisions that the week before would have been unthinkable. When would a funeral be held? Who would officiate? Which mortuary? We must choose caskets, a burial plot. On and on decisions needed to be made. Fortunately, friends and family made many for me. Jack chose a funeral home with which he was acquainted. The mortician showed us the beautiful expensive caskets he had. Jack took over and said, "My brother would not want anything fancy or expensive. We will choose the simplest gray caskets." I requested one gray casket for Dick and one for the boys, who were to be placed together. Grandpa and Grandma decided to purchase enough plots in the local cemetery for themselves as well as for Dick and the boys.

My parents and brothers and sisters came to support me.

Which minister? Grandpa and Grandma attended the church in Auburn. I, of course, did not know the pastor. When we lived in Bakersfield, California and attended the Hillcrest church, Pastor Krick, a godly and caring man, had been our pastor. He was retired and living in northern California. I asked him if he would officiate, and he consented. Pallbearers were selected from among Dick's friends.

How does one explain to an eight-year-old girl what had happened? This was probably very inadequately done. We went together to the funeral home and the mortician showed us open and closed caskets. I attempted to explain to Carmen that Daddy, Richie, and Rodney would be put in caskets like these; the lid would be closed, and they would be buried. She was probably unable to process much of what I told her. Because they had been burned when the plane went down, we could not see them. This made it easy to think it didn't really happen.

How does one describe the emotional trauma of a funeral? Fortunately, someone had recently given me a black suit, so at least I did not have to go shopping to dress appropriately.

When the mortuary vehicle arrived to transport us to the church, I wanted to run and hide. I cringed at the thought of going through with this, but running away was not possible. This was happening, and I was a part of it, as much as I did not want to be. The chapel was full of flowers given by friends and family. To this day, I cannot tolerate the heavy perfume of flowers; it means a funeral.

Then it was on to a brief ceremony at the graveside where I kissed the caskets goodbye, leaving them to rest on the hill above Auburn. The final "ceremony" of the day was a dinner at the Auburn church prepared by the church members so my guests would have an opportunity to come and talk with me. I am unable to express how wonderful friends and family are on such a painful day. Nor can I count the multiple acts of kindness we enjoyed—gifts of food, phone calls, letters, cards, and more.

The memorial money collected from family and friends was given to build a country chapel on Secundino's farm in the mountains above Matagalpa. God had painfully answered our prayers for a church. I knew Dick and the boys would approve if they had known.

Though many painful decisions had been made, there were still more to make. Home, work, and life with friends in Nicaragua were now relegated to my past. I still had the VW van that needed to be taken to Nicaragua. What would I do with that? Tom and Nancy, student missionaries in Nicaragua the year before, offered to drive the VW to Hospital Adventista de Nicaragua. It was so thoughtful of them to take the time to do that.

Then I had to deal with so many "things." We had purchased supplies we would need when we returned to Nicaragua, and much of it must be cared for. Most of it was given to others who could use it. There was also a houseful of things in Nicaragua to be disposed of. There was nothing there important enough for me to go back and get. Pat Sparks, the doctor's wife and also a friend from college, took on the task. I attempted to make a list of everything in the house with a price. She sold those things to people in the area. There were a few things with which I was not yet ready to part, so she packed those up and sent them to me. In retrospect, I should have had her sell everything, as the stuff was seriously damaged in shipment.

The biggest decision was, "What was I going to do now?" Carmen and I had no place to call home. We had nothing familiar around us to help us put our lives together—not a pillow of our own, not a favorite doll or teddy for Carmen to hold. All that was familiar were the few things we had in our suitcases. Our situation was almost like that of a war refugee or a displaced family.

The GC generously assisted with funeral expenses, and granted me Dick's salary for six months, but where would I live? My sister Shirley invited us to stay with them at Blue Mountain Academy in Pennsylvania to give me time to adjust and decide what to do next. I accepted her offer, and my parents volunteered to drive us across the country to their home. So we left Dick's family in Auburn with an empty house and with the task of picking up the pieces of their lives. In a few days, we were again at my family home in Ruthven, Iowa. After leaving Ruthven, we traveled on to Pennsylvania with an uncharted future, and my parents returned to their home at the farm and to their own struggles with sorrow.

Chapter 12

Remembering Them

The air was cold and crisp that December morning in Pennsylvania. I had been there only a month. I was bundled up for my walk—my time to think and to pray.

I stepped out into a scene of breath-taking beauty. Snow covered the drabness of winter, and ice glazed the snow. Each blade of grass, each twig on the bushes, and all the trees sparkled like a crystalline jewels in the sunshine. I must call photographer Dick to get pictures of this. Call him? That was no longer possible. Grief almost overwhelmed me. Beauty is to be shared, and the one with whom I could most enjoy it was gone.

My Father, my Lord, my heavenly friend, the maker of beauty, my heart is as cold as this ice. You gave me everything my heart desired. At the funeral Pastor Krick read a few paragraphs that I had written about my family, and closed by quoting Job 1:21, "Naked I came from my mother's womb, and naked I will depart. The LORD gave and the LORD has taken away; may the name of the LORD be praised" (NIV).

You gave me so much, and now most of it is gone. Father, how can I go on living without them? The refiner's fire (Isa. 48:10) is more than I can bear. What do You wish to refine out of my character?

Father, you gave me so much. First, You gave me a husband when I had no anticipation of getting married, but planned to serve you in Burma as a single person. Life was an adventure living with Dick. He was so full of life and enjoyed so many things. How can I describe him? Kind, loving, generous, always wanting to go places and do things, he kept my life very interesting. His joy of music, both participating in it and listening to it, greatly enriched my life. He loved to be out of doors, camping, hiking, exploring the unknown, even as I did. He was the spiritual leader of our home, initiating worships together even before we were married. He loved people and so much enjoyed doing things with friends, but he especially relished singing with others. As a teacher, he took some difficult punches in life, but he never held a grudge. Father, you also gave me a husband who knew how to do things, fix things, and build things. He was someone whom I could depend on. We did have one point of friction, though, which required adjustments. Dick was from "mañana" land, and I had grown up trained to be always on time. But You took care of our differences, for, gradually, he learned to be more punctual, and I learned to relax a bit.

Then you gave us Richie. How a baby changes a home! What a pleasure it was to be a parent and watch this little baby grow and develop physically, mentally, and spiritually. He was only three when our pastor gave a series of Wednesday evening prayer meeting on last-day events and the soon coming of Jesus. We went to each one. He did not wiggle and squirm, but sat quietly and listened in rapt attention. Lord, you know he loved You. You gave him a keen mind and a desire for learning. How he loved the various pets we had, watching the bees in the bee hive that Dick had put outside his window, so he could observe them. He also loved to build and create things and was developing a talent for writing poetry and water painting. We took him everywhere with us, even to the beach when he was just a few weeks old, and hiking in the mountains when he was carried in a back pack. He was the joy of our lives.

How excited Richie was when he knew he was to have a little brother or sister. What a beautiful baby she was and what a joy it was to watch her develop. Carmen loved her dolls, and was always an incurable mommy. Richie soon had someone to play with, and they spent many happy hours together.

Then Rodney came to join our family. He soon showed his personality as a fun-loving little boy who kept us laughing. He had interesting names for many things, like roads were "jiggledy-jaggidy roads." A friend once asked me how I could keep a straight face long enough to discipline him. When Carmen thought up something fun to do, he happily took her hand, for he knew she would lead them into new adventures.

Yes, Father, you richly blessed me with a wonderful family. I so much enjoyed the profession of being a wife and mother and homemaker. We did so many things together, including working for the church in both volunteering and employment. You gave purpose to our lives as we committed ourselves to serve You. We committed our children to you and taught them the joy of serving you.

So Father, you filled my cup to overflowing, and now it seems almost empty. I thank you for Carmen, but how can I now raise her without her father, without her brothers? How can I raise her as a joyous child, when I no longer have joy?

Father, you have guided my life thus far, and I believe that You will continue to do so, but You will need to carry me for a while because now I am only going through the motions of living. I trust You to show me how You want me to live the remainder of my life with so much missing. Refine out of my character whatever needs to be refined. Give me employment to provide for our physical needs. Keep me close to You.

Thank You for the beauty of this morning, and please carry me through this day.

Your hurting daughter, Iris

Chapter 13

Restoring My Soul

Shirley found a way to adjust her house to accommodate two more people. Carmen went to school, and I walked many hours on the wintry roads trying to sort out what had happened. How does one continue living when life has ended and the heart is dead? Why had this happened? Where was God in this? The mental struggles were exhausting; it took so much work to grieve.

In a short time, I realized there was no answer to the question "Why?" and to stay on that track would lead to mental illness.

One story haunted me. It was the story of a lady who had a wonderful husband, a lovely home, and stalwart sons. The older sons were teenagers and the youngest was only a baby. They lived on a farm not far from a river. Life was good. Then came a flood. They all tried to find good places to hang on above the water level. Tragically one-by-one her husband and sons were swept away and drowned. She managed to hang on while holding the baby in one arm. She told of the pain, but then she added something that caused her even greater pain. That baby grew up and chose the wrong path. He was put in prison for life. That heartache was far worse than the death of her husband and older sons. No one knows the future. We'd like to think all will turn out well, but could that have happened to my family? I wanted to believe it would not have, but it was a possibility.

Some family members told me they came back to the Lord because of what happened to my family. Would they have come back anyway? I gave up on the puzzle, knowing the answer would only be found in heaven.

Where was God in all of this? He had protected us over and over again in dangerous situations. We had seen God lead us step by step. Why not this time? Under the pressure of our schedule, Dick had taken off when advised not to, but God could have used any number of methods to stop him from doing so. Certainly God was strong enough to handle things even when we don't listen well.

Had God forsaken me? No, God had been my friend too many years for me to believe that. The brush on my arm that I experienced the day of the accident, I believe, was my angel touching me to tell me that God was with me.

Searching for answers, I turned to the writings of Ellen White who also lost two sons and her husband. How did she respond? After all this, how did she reach out to others? I found much comfort in her writings, but perhaps her insight is best summed up in the following statement: "The blessed Saviour stands by many whose eyes are so blinded by tears that they do not discern Him. He longs to clasp our hands, to have us look to Him in simple faith, permitting Him to guide us. His heart is open to our griefs, our sorrows, and our trials. He has loved us with an everlasting love and with loving-kindness compassed us about. We may keep the heart stayed upon Him and meditate on His loving-kindness all the day. He will lift the soul above the daily sorrow and perplexity, into a realm of peace" (*Thoughts from the Mount of Blessing*, p, 12).

I remembered Biblical examples of loss and grief. David, Job and many others cried out to God for answers. When they realized the greatness and holiness of God, they questioned no more, and realized that in the end, God would make all things right. To God, the important thing is not how long a person lives. Instead, a person's eternal destiny is most important. Hezekiah is an example of an unwillingness to accept death. Rather than remain focused on God and using his extra years to glorify God and thank Him for renewed health, he became proud of his wealth and showed it to the Babylonians. (Notably, during Hezekiah's extra 15 years, the wicked Manasseh was born to him (2 Kings 20 and 21), the same Manasseh who was included in Jesus' lineage [Matt. 1:10].)

God had blessed me with 13 years of being a part of a happy, loving, and adventuresome family. Nobody could steal those memories; they were forever mine. Many people had never had the privilege of making such memories.

Little-by-little God gave me peace and helped me trust in Him, but I still wondered if He could revive a dead heart. What should I do from here? Emotionally, I had lost both arms and a leg. Those could never be replaced. Was adapting possible? I realized it was time to look at my options.

The easiest way out would be suicide. If I believed, as many Christians do, that there is immediate life in heaven after death, it would be logical to die and join my husband and my boys. Fortunately, I believed my family was sleeping in the grave. Suicide would be murder, and the Ten Commandments prohibited that (Exod. 20:13). (I do not believe that all suicides are murder. Some are due to mental illness. God will be the judge.) And what about my daughter? To lose me also would not be fair to her. That option was crossed off.

One consideration caused me some anger toward God: Why had the accident happened to only three of our family and not to all of us? We had traveled thousands of miles together. Why didn't an accident happen when we were all together? Surely it would have not hurt my larger family any more to lose all of the family rather than a part. The pain of continuing to live seemed at times just too great and the need to refocus life too difficult.

Another option I thought about was to lose my grief by living in an unreal world of reading novels or perhaps I could take drugs to numb my pain? Reading was my hobby. How easy it would be to not face life by going down that road. Was that what I wanted? Was that what God would like? I decided it was not because I knew I would come to hate myself.

I could fall into self-pity and depend on others to continue to support me. Family and friends were kind and gracious, but soon they would not want me around. Welfare was distasteful. With my nursing profession, I knew it was possible for me to make a living.

The last option was the only one that appealed to me—to bury my heartache deep and live a productive life earning a living and helping others. I reckoned that emotional limbs cannot be replaced any more than physical ones can. Since my own mother, and Uncle Ted, and other crippled people, had learned to live with their handicaps, I could too, though I knew it would not be easy.

I decided it was time to be involved and get busy, but where would I go and what kind of nursing did I want to do? I prayed that God would lead me. At the time when I made this resolve, I didn't realize how important it would be. Through the ensuing years, work became the way I handled the emotional pain. When I was busy, I found it easier to forget my losses.

In late January (maybe February) a phone call came with a surprising request. The girls' dean at an academy in New Jersey had found it necessary to resign, and the principal was searching for a new dean. Would I come and complete the year? I considered his request seriously, but realizing my emotional handicap, decided it would not be a good fit. The answer was, "No."

My sister, Rosy, had been Alice Smith's executive secretary for many years. When I was teaching at Columbia Union College, I had suggested Rosy's name to Alice Smith, the dean of the nursing school. She had hired Rosy as her executive secretary. Now Rosy desired to return that favor and be supportive of me. She suggested we find a place of employment in a hospital where she could start a new career doing medical records, and where I could be a nurse. Possibilities opened up. God led us to the hospital in Menard, Texas. There Rosy would work in medical records, and I would be assistant administrator for nursing. The hospital was owned by the county and operated by Adventists. Rosy had a son at home to consider, and I had a daughter. A small church school would meet their educational needs. Early in the spring, Shirley and her family drove Carmen and me all the way to Texas to begin the next phase of our lives. Never will I be able to thank them enough for what they did for me. Rosy and her son, Doug, joined us after the completion of his school year.

The reader might ask questions about how I handled my grief. Why did I not go to grief counseling? Frankly, that possibility never occurred to me. I don't remember that there were any supportive grief recovery groups available then. If there were, I was not aware of them. Being in a rural area, there probably were none.

The two mechanisms I used to deal with grief were (1) work, and (2) blocking memories. The first was intentional. When I was busy, I didn't have time to think. It also fit the work ethic I had learned as a child—no minute should be wasted. The second was unintentional. Until years later, I really didn't realize how much blocking I had done. Many years after the accident, I decided to put together a book for Carmen with pictures and narration. Only by looking at the pictures did some memories return. I observed that the memories that brought me pain were gone.

I might add here one of my reactions. After the accident I wanted nothing to do with small, private planes. If I had my way, no one would ever catch me in one of those again!

Looking back, it is evident to me that God's Holy Spirit had patiently counseled and comforted me in my mental turmoil.

Did I go through the recognized "stages of grief?" Actually, I didn't. They didn't seem to apply to the way I felt. For years, and perhaps even now, certain incidents make it feel like I am reliving the week of the accident. A song Dick used to sing, a child who looks like one of my sons, pictures, special occasions, and other experiences can unexpectedly trigger overwhelming grief. One day in Menard, a five-year-old boy came in for a tonsillectomy. I was the circulating nurse that day. The little boy looked so much like Rodney that I had a hard time keeping it together enough to function.

So did I heal? That depends on how one defines healing. The wound is buried under scar tissue. If "healing" means being able to enjoy some things and having some direction in life, the answer is, "yes."

Gradually, I became more productive in my work. One lovely, spring morning about a year and a half after the accident when I was walking to work, I felt joy at the beauty around me. Suddenly, I realized that this was the first time I had felt that way since the accident. I could hardly believe what was happening to me. I asked myself, "Can I actually enjoy life again and not just go through the motions of living?" The thought was exhilarating.

One spin-off of my experience was that it left me with a sense that there are relatively few things in life worth fighting for or that deserve getting overly concerned about. I had lost almost everything important and had survived. When small, negative things happen, I keep them in perspective by asking, "Would I even remember this incident in a year?"

Although we were busy in Menard, we took time for fun. Nursing had taught me that no human can heal their own body, mind, or soul; however, people can intentionally place themselves in situations where healing occurs. For us, this included excursions into the great outdoors. There were state parks where we went camping. Big Bend National Park was close enough for us to enjoy many a weekend. The church went camping at a park where there was a river. In that restful, delightful setting, Carmen made her decision to be baptized. Along with others, she was baptized in the sparkling river flowing though the camp. More than any day since the accident, my heart sang. How I wished Dick and the boys could have shared that event with us. Dick would have been so proud of Carmen.

After living in Menard for over three years, I faced the fact that my nursing profession was what was gave me focus in life, and that I needed more education so I could advance in my career. It was time to go back to school to earn a master's degree. Carmen also needed a different social environment, something more than Menard offered. Rosy, too, was ready to move on professionally. Rosy chose to go to Loma Linda University in California, but somehow, living in Loma Linda had never appealed to me. In discussing educational possibilities with nursing leaders, it was suggested that it would be good for the diversity of Adventist nursing if I went to a non-Adventist university. I chose the University of Washington in Seattle. Convergence had happened in our family; a change would be good for all of us.

The three and a half years of working in Menard had given me time to find direction for my life. The loss of my family would always hurt, but I could sense that God was restoring my soul. By now, I knew myself well enough to realize that work, study, and becoming involved with life would soften the hurt. Later in my life I would take another step, one of learning to sit quietly and meditate on the wonders of God's nature.

Could I have foreseen my future at that time, I would have been amazed to know that God would someday make me a world traveler and help me start a nursing school. I would have laughed at the thought of Iris being held at gunpoint and surviving; of somehow managing a missed flight in Nigeria when all the planes were full; and of dealing with a leaky gas tank when driving around Africa with a car filled only with women. For now, though, I still needed to be busy. God had prepared me to tackle the next challenge. The other events would come in their own course.

Chapter 14
Nicaraguan Graduation

It was another Sabbath afternoon in Nicaragua. But this time I was not surveying the campus of Hospital Adventista de Nicaragua from my own front room window. No, I was there on another errand and staying in the guest room. Permit me to backtrack a few months and offer an explanation.

While we were still in Menard, Texas, an unexpected letter came from Nicaragua. The graduating nursing class requested I come and participate in their graduation. This was the same class I had taught when they were freshman.

How time had vanished! Were Carmen and I ready to go back to Nicaragua? We talked it over and decided we would go. So, I accepted the invitation, and we found ourselves boarding a plane to Managua.

That was both a good trip and a difficult one. The students were eager to show us the tree that had been planted in Dick's honor. We expressed appreciation, knowing that nothing would so please Dick as to be remembered by a beautiful mango tree. Of course, someone else was living in our home, but being back on campus brought back many good memories of what had been, and it helped to provide closure to that chapter in my life. It also gave us opportunity to visit old friends.

Graduation was wonderful. How the students had matured during that time! I was so proud of them and felt so honored to be part of this important step in their lives. In a way, it was my own graduation, too, for it symbolized a milepost in my personal growth. Little did I know that I was soon to venture off as a single parent into an unknown world, more alone than I had ever been before—without parents, without Adventist teachers and classmates, without sisters, without a husband. I had accepted my widowhood and was ready to take another step forward professionally. Even having the courage to travel to Nicaragua with Carmen signaled a change in me.

Mazie Herin was at the graduation representing the nursing section of the GC Health Department. I greatly admired Mazie. She had been Dean of the Union College School of

Nursing and had been instrumental in shifting Adventist nursing education from being hospital-based to being college-based. I shared my intentions with her of going back to school and expressed indecision over where to apply. She counseled me that while Loma Linda was an excellent school, perhaps it would be wise for me to attend a state university to receive an education that would broaden Adventist nursing. Though she would not advise many people to do this, she believed I was spiritually mature enough to handle the challenges I would face in a public university. I took her counsel seriously, feeling God had arranged this divine appointment for me.

As Carmen and I boarded the plane leaving Managua, we did not know this would truly be our last-ever chance to visit Nicaragua, nor did we have an inkling of the seismic events that would soon shake Nicaragua. The next day, the very day after we left, a massive earthquake devastated Managua. Not long after that, a political revolution shook the country. Nicaragua became a communist country and Hospital Adventista de Nicaragua was taken over by Cuban doctors.

We had planned our trip so we could visit friends in Mexico on the way home. We enjoyed our time with them, but we had trouble at the airport when we tried to leave. The immigration officer in Mexico City did not want me to leave the country with Carmen. He stated that she needed her father's permission to travel out of the country. That was a painful experience because it was the first time I had to explain to anyone (and in Spanish) that Carmen's father was not living. Fortunately, I finally convinced him, and we were allowed to make our way back to Texas to prepare for our move to Seattle.

Chapter 15

Nothing Lacking, Seattle

Armed with Mazie's advice, I applied for—and was accepted into—a master's program at the University of Washington in Seattle, Washington.

As a single parent without assistance from any family member, I had to consider well the needs of Carmen. After working 60 to 70 hours a week in Menard, Texas, and often having to change plans for the needs of the hospital, I asked the GC if they would be willing to give me sustentation until Carmen completed the eighth grade. They granted my request to back me financially for three and a half years. With that support, and with what I had saved, I could go to school without working. That would allow me to concentrate on my schooling and still care for Carmen.

The first concern was housing. The Grahams, friends of Dick from college days, took us in until we could find housing and until the moving van arrived. Considering my options, I decided to buy. We found a home in Kirkland with a low-interest loan and payments low enough to handle. The best advantage was that the house was within walking distance of the Adventist school. As Carmen made friends, she was delighted to discover that her friends were within easy walking distance.

Another plus of this Kirkland home was that it was an easy commute to the University of Washington. Our home was not far from the floating bridge that crossed Lake Washington. Once I crossed the floating bridge, the university was only about a half mile up the hill. At first I drove to school, but I soon found that the drive could be eternal in the mornings. Then, to my joy, a bus stop was added just below the university, so all I needed to do was drive a short distance from home to a Park-and-Ride, board the bus, and relax on the way to school. (Dick had spoiled me by doing most of the driving and by taking care of a car. I never found much pleasure in those tasks.) The walk up the hill to the university was good for me. I didn't complain except when the weather was too inclement.

It had been my expectation that I should be able to complete my master's degree in Community Health Nursing in the allotted three years, taking only 8-10 hours of class work each quarter. Unfortunately, when I arrived on campus, it was discovered that the Bachelor of Science program I had taken at Walla Walla did not include any classes in Community Health Nursing. Ouch! I did not have adequate undergraduate hours to qualify for the master degree I wanted. The only way I could enter that master's program was to first take the University of Washington's Bachelor of Science program for diploma nurses. I was not pleased.

The next hurdle concerned the length of time I had been out of school. Although I had taken basic sciences at Emmanuel Mission College (Andrew's University) as part of pre-nursing, that had been more than 10 years hence. The University of Washington found it too ancient to accept.

The verdict was that I needed to take anatomy and physiology, microbiology, chemistry, plus my BS nursing subjects. How upset I was! I had taught medical/surgical nursing, and I did not like the thought of taking it again as a student. It meant that rather than taking 8-10 hours a quarter, I would now need to take 16-18 hours a quarter, and I would not have as much time with Carmen as I had planned.

There was some good news, though. The chemistry teacher said that if I passed the final test, he would verify that my chemistry knowledge was up-to-date. I studied, and with the help of the Lord, managed to pass that test. The microbiology teacher did not require that I take the lab, and yes, I could take advanced credit exams for my nursing subjects and thus eliminate one quarter. However, they specified that in order to eliminate that quarter's study, I could not pick and choose to challenge only the classes about which I felt most confident, rather, I must be tested on all the scheduled classes for the quarter involved. Thankfully, I successfully completed those exams (whew!), and my counselor and I made a schedule for me to be able to complete the master's degree in the three years.

After some time, I lost my annoyance at having to take this much education, for many of the professors were excellent teachers. Since I had been a student, the electron microscope had been discovered, and physiology was almost a new subject. The medical-surgical nursing professor was one of the best. She taught this subject in a very different way from what I had been taught, so it was a pleasure to take her class. Association with other students as we struggled through classes together added zest to my life.

When I was finally able to register for the master's program, I opted to specifically target my interest in health education in developing countries, and I registered for my electives in those classes. Interestingly, community health nursing seemed to be going out of vogue then. All the other students in that department were taking the nurse practitioner pathway. My counselor tried to persuade me to do the same, but I was not interested in becoming a nurse practitioner. So, in one of my classes, I was the only student. The instructor, understandably, was not particularly interested in teaching only one student, so it was one of the poorest classes I took. By contrast, in my psychology class there were about 800 students. It was an excellent class.

When Carmen saw the long hours I put in on class work, she vowed she would never get a master's degree; it was too much work. I did, indeed, spend a lot of time on it, especially in finishing my thesis.

Carmen settled into school, dealing with all the ups and downs of progressing through grades 5 to 8. We joined Pathfinders (I was a counselor) and together we enjoyed many outings and activities with them. We treasured our time in Washington with all the school and church activities, the beautiful mountains, and other attractions of the area. I thought Washington might be a good place to live permanently.

One of the older students in Carmen's school died suddenly. The student wasn't a particularly close friend, but Carmen cried uncontrollably at the funeral. I thought that perhaps she was finally grieving for our family, and I felt this opportunity to cry with her friends was therapeutic for her. Unfortunately, Carmen's teacher told the students that the cause of death was the flu. For some time Carmen worried that she would get the flu and die.

Carmen has grown into a young lady ready to graduate from the eighth grade.

At last I completed my master's in community health nursing, and Carmen was soon to graduate from the eighth grade. Seattle had an adequate supply of nurses, so it would be necessary for me to look for employment elsewhere. I recognized that another change would be very difficult for Carmen because she had formed some very meaningful friendships in Kirkland. In watching Carmen's development, I concluded that to be well-rounded, she needed more male adult companionship than it was possible for me to offer as a single parent. A possible way to do this would be to place her in a boarding school situation.

My employment options narrowed down to two: to be director of the nursing school in Fletcher, North Carolina, or to be director of Proyecto Adventista de Nutricion (with the acronym "PAN," an appropriate name as "pan" is "bread" in Spanish) at Hospital Adventista, Valle de Angeles, Honduras. I had worked with graduates of Fletcher and believed it was an excellent school. However, it was a diploma school, and I realized that diploma schools were being phased out. I talked with the administrator of the hospital in Fletcher, and he said that he would call me on a certain day to hear my decision. This was a very difficult decision to make. What was the future of the nursing school at Fletcher?

What schooling opportunities would there be for Carmen? On the other hand, how could I go to Honduras and leave Carmen in the United States? I battled with my thoughts. Oh, how I wished Dick were there to help me make the decision.

All of the processes I had learned for decision making did not work in this case. There were too many unknowns. Seasons of prayer did not seem to give me the answer. I found myself doing something that I had never done before. Turning to my Heavenly Father, I asked him to give me a sign as to what I should do. If the administrator from Fletcher phoned on the day he said he would, I would go to Fletcher. If he did not, I would accept that as an indication that I should accept the call to Honduras. I felt at peace.

So I waited. What would be the outcome? The day came when the phone call was due. The administrator did not call. In fact, it wasn't until about five days later that he phoned. He explained that they had an emergency and finding a director for the nursing school had been put on the back burner. I told him I was sorry, but I had accepted the invitation to go to Honduras. What happened to the nursing school in Fletcher? Sometime later I was told that within a relatively short time, it closed. If I had accepted that call, I would have been dean of a dying school, and Carmen would have been uprooted at least one more time. As for Carmen, Campion Academy in Colorado seemed the best choice for a school.

My friends couldn't believe I had made such a decision. Some tried to dissuade me. Doubts set in. But I was assured that God had given me a sign of His will, and I knew I would be happiest if I followed His leading. There was nothing I could say to explain my decision to my friends and convince them that it was a wise choice. Preparations were made for this major move. I shopped for things I would need, sold items I would not need, and separated items into the ones to be shipped to Colorado and the ones to be shipped to Honduras. Carmen and I enjoyed our last trips to the mountains, to Seattle, and to the ocean. The house sold quickly, and we packed up. Final tearful goodbyes were said, and we and our things were on our way. How difficult it was to say goodbye to our friends there. Carmen and I both still miss the friends we made in Seattle.

 My sister, Grace, lived in Denver, and she agreed to meet me at the airport when I came to Denver in exchange for the use of my car. The administration in Honduras consented to my request to go to Denver whenever I needed, but at my own expense. I anticipated I would return each Thanksgiving, Christmas, and spring break.

I purchased a single-wide mobile home in Loveland, Colorado and settled our things there so we would have a "home" when I came back to visit. We arranged for my cousin Rita to live in it and care for it for me. However, I learned that Campion gave their students home-leave weekends once a month. They no longer had the schedule to which I was accustomed. Now how could that be managed?

We settled Carmen into the dormitory, and then I had to leave. She seemed so young and vulnerable. It was heart-wrenching when Carmen and I told each other goodbye. We had torn up our roots in Kirkland, and once again we both faced new situations and new friends. In fact, we both faced totally new environments, this time without each other. How would this work?

As I had asked God to make this decision for me, I trusted Him that this would be best for both of us. After leaving Carmen, I drove back to Denver. Grace to took me to the airport, and I was on my way to an unknown life, while Carmen was starting her life in a new school. As it turned out, God came through for Carmen. She prospered in all areas of her life. She especially enjoyed the ski trips at Campion.

CHAPTER 16

My Cup Runs Over, Honduras

Flying into Tegucigalpa, Honduras is a challenge for any pilot because Tegucigalpa is surrounded by rugged mountains. Flying was never something I did for pleasure, for nearly always when the plane descended, my stomach stayed in the air and left a deposit in that little white bag. Happily, once I landed, my stomach settled down.

Airports are important to missionaries, and this one was no exception. The hospital staff looked forward to meeting flights not only to welcome newcomers but to watch the planes come and go. Old friends met me when I arrived in Honduras. Doctors Frank and Janet McNiel had worked at the hospital in Nicaragua when Dick and I worked there, and I had briefly met Ron and JoAnn McBroom in Guatemala when we traveled there on our way to Nicaragua. It was a pleasure to see them again.

A winding gravel road took us out of the valley and up to Valle de Angeles to the campus of Hospital Adventista de Honduras. The mountainsides were covered with pine trees festooned with air plants. The roads could be a challenge because during the heavy rainy season the water washed heavy ruts into the gravel road. Much to the relief of the hospital staff, this road was eventually blacktopped.

Proyecto Adventista de Nutricion was funded by EZE, which stands for Evangelische Zentralstelle, the Protestant Association for Cooperation in Development, a German church-based development organization. The project aimed at bettering the nutrition of the people in the surrounding area. To meet this goal, we planned classes in nutrition, education on providing a clean home environment, and training so the people would learn how to grow gardens. Because of their poverty, we also wanted to help train them so they would be able to buy adequate food and support themselves. It was envisioned that the women could earn money through the making of crafts and selling them. What a challenge! The EZE grant included funding for erecting a building which would include space for the director's home, for offices, and for a meeting hall with a demonstration kitchen.

Oh, yes, since transportation was necessary, a truck was included in the proposal, but that request had been denied. Instead, they approved the purchase of three motorcycles, Yamaha 125s. I didn't know whether to laugh or cry at the thought of Iris riding a motorcycle! I knew too well that motorcycles were dangerous because my own brother had nearly lost his life on one. Besides, I was not well-coordinated. This challenge was going to take special intervention from God, but again He came through. I was never injured on the motorcycle, and I never wiped out anyone else. To get my motorcycle license, Ron McBroom, the hospital administrator, simply appeared at the motor vehicle department and paid the fee. Apparently, the vehicle department had no idea what kind of a driver they were endorsing.

When I arrived, the hospital was still very much in the process of development. The McNiels had started the work by opening a clinic in a house in the village. Gradually, the hospital grew. The first building housed the clinic, lab, a business office, and a kitchen. Homes were built some distance away; though housing was usually in short supply. As new staff members were added, new homes were built. When I arrived, the clinic wing of the hospital was well established, and work was continuing on the in-patient wings. Church was held in the lobby of the clinic.

The EZE building was still only on paper. As there was no place for me to live, I stayed in the guest room in the McBroom's house. It soon became apparent that it would be a long time before the EZE building would become a reality. What was I going to do about this? Since there was a new home in the village that was available for rent, this became my home and the PAN center. My living room would also serve as a meeting hall and as the headquarters for the project. Unfortunately, the house was directly across the street from "city hall," and the mayor liked to play music on speakers loud enough so his whole village could hear. This often disturbed me, but I learned that one can learn to block out extraneous noises, if necessary.

Over time, the program developed, taking on an emphasis of serving moms and their children. We weighed the children and provided classes for the moms. In this way, we identified a large number of malnourished children. It became obvious there were insufficient resources in the homes to change this. In the culture of the area, available food was given first to the father, then to the mother, then to the children beginning with the eldest. This often left the smallest ones with little or nothing. A sad advertising campaign pictured a baby on boxes of inexpensive corn starch, suggesting that mixing it with water in a bottle made good baby food.

We decided to apply for U.S. government CARE (which stands for Cooperative for

Assistance and Relief Everywhere, an American-based private international humanitarian organization) food to be given to families with malnourished children. Our proposal was accepted. This drew many more families to the meetings. As would be expected, much of the CARE food went to the father, not to the malnourished children! An amazing thing happened, however. The father was energized to work harder, and the lot of the whole family improved, including the small children. To see these improvements was gratifying.

A typical kitchen in the village.

My staff soon added two more nurses and a man whose job it was to promote agriculture. As the project grew, we wanted to hold meetings in many locations so the moms did not have to walk so far with their little children. Clearly, we needed proper transportation to carry the equipment and food. I personally purchased a simple Toyota pickup (it didn't even have a heater) that served us well. From the beginning, it was understood that it belonged to the hospital, but I could use it as mine as long as I needed it.

Rather than ride the motorcycle, I often walked over the mountains to visit the homes. This is what the local people did, and I found I was better accepted when I did too. After much practice, one of the other nurses learned to ride a motorcycle, but the other nurse never tried. The agricultural man used the third motorcycle most of the time.

Eventually the planned EZE building was completed, and we had a place to work more effectively. At the entrance there was a demonstration garden which was useful for teaching and for providing food, and it also added beauty to the center. To round out the staff, a local gardener and a maid were hired to care for the garden and keep the center clean.

A slat house was added for selling plants, as well as selling the macramé crafts the ladies had made. Some of the ladies were taught to make banana bread that they sold to people coming to the clinic. It was a challenge to help them understand that the bread must be fresh when they sold it, and in order for the macramé to sell, the knots must all be tied correctly.

One of the homes I visited. With an alcoholic husband and the community pigs eating her garden, she had a struggle.

The project also provided pedal sewing machines. It was difficult to teach the ladies how to sew, since most of them had never even held a pair of scissors. Sometimes we taught sewing classes at the PAN center; other times we took the sewing machines to a larger home some distance from the hospital and left them there during the weeks we taught classes. At first, some of the people were not friendly to our program and only reluctantly consented to have classes in their home. However, when they saw how we were helping the people, they became more friendly and supportive.

A scarlet macaw named Kathy enlivened my life. Kathy spent most of her days on the garden fence. In the evening she perched on a "T" pole in my house. In the mornings if I did not wake up as early as she thought I should, she would slide down the pole and bang her beak on the bed to wake me. She melted my heart when she would climb on my lap and caress my cheeks. The negative part was having to clip her wings. Reportedly, pet macaws can be allowed freedom to fly wherever they want, and they will always return home, but the likelihood of Kathy being shot was great enough that I kept her wings clipped. Occasionally on Sabbaths I would take my bird and go to the river a few miles away and spend some quiet time reading, watching the birds,

Kathy on the garden fence in front of the PAN center.

writing letters, or just meditating. I found I needed this quiet time to recoup my emotional resources.

When I was in Honduras, I was asked to be a delegate to a Union session held in Costa Rica. The Houghton family we had known in Bluefields, Nicaragua was there with their three children. It was a treat to see them, but I was totally unprepared for how I would react at seeing their children, the ones who had played with mine and who were about the same age. I thought I was healing from my losses, but on that day, I fell apart. As soon as I could, I sought a quiet place to be alone, to cry, and to pray.

As planned, I often returned to Denver and then drove on to Loveland to spend time with Carmen. For longer vacations, she came to Honduras. The first summer she visited Honduras, I purchased a smaller motorcycle (a Yamaha 90) for her, so she could go various places with me. She also accompanied others on little excursions. The next summer, however, she decided to work at the youth camp in Colorado and enjoyed it so much that she spent several more summers serving at youth camps. Fortunately, she had some substitute parents on campus who were a tremendous help to her while she was at Campion. Often friends invited her to visit their homes on weekend leaves. God had been faithful in caring for the one most dear to me. My heart praised Him for this!

Grace, my sister in Denver, made many trips to the airport to pick up or send off one or the other of us. I really appreciate what she did for us. We always felt welcome in her home.

Back at Campion Carmen had grown into a lovely young lady. She had decided to go to Union College to study nursing after graduation Campion. When I was coming to the GC during her senior year, she still wished to go to Union College to be near her friends.

A group from Hinsdale Hospital came down to help complete the hospital wing. When it was finished, we were able to admit patients. Ron had pictures framed and hung, which made the hospital look truly finished. Then it was time for the dedication. Elder Wilson, GC president then, and other representatives from the GC, from the Inter-American Division, and from the Central American Union came to preside over the ceremonies. This was an especially joyful day for Elder Folkenberg, who had conceived the idea of this hospital in Honduras and had raised funds for its building.

Although we did not talk about religion in our health education program, the combined efforts of all the departments caused the church to grow. How God blessed us! The project was funded for three years. When that time was completed, EZE did not grant a renewal of the funding. The administration had not seriously discussed with me what would happen to the project or to my job, so I was a bit uneasy about my future, but as it turned out, it became clear that God hadn't forgotten me.

My father was ill, and I made a quick trip stateside to Ruthven, Iowa to visit my parents. While there, someone called on the phone and requested to talk with me. The message shocked me. It had been voted by the Seventh-day Adventist General Conference Executive Committee to invite me to come to the GC to join the Church's Health and Temperance Department. I would be an associate director with the responsibility of world nursing. Surely, they had gotten the wrong name! What expertise did I have to offer the world field? I told the caller, "I'll think and pray about it, and I'll let you know." I don't remember who phoned, but perhaps it was Elder Baasch because he was then the Associate Secretary with responsibility for the Inter-American Division.

My father had been the strength of our family. It was difficult to see him ill.

Many people would have seen this as a great opportunity; however, since both my mother's cousin and brother had worked in the GC for many years, it held no illusions of glamour for me. I thought it sounded like work, plain and simple. It meant countless committees and endless travel. Besides, I had lived in the Washington D.C. area when Dick was taking his master's program, and I didn't want to move back there to city living.

My mind was in turmoil. I believed I needed a doctorate for that position. I greatly admired Mazie Herin who had been in that position for many years. Lois Burnett, who had held the position before Mazie, was also an esteemed educator and had started a nursing school in the Philippines after leaving the GC. The one vacating the position was Ruth White, equally qualified as a nursing educator. How could I fill the enormous shoes of these dedicated leaders of Adventist nursing? I thought about my current work in Honduras. It had probably been the most satisfying work I had ever done in my nursing profession. Could I leave it at this stage? If only I could discuss the matter with Dick. After much time in prayer, the Lord impressed me that this is what I should do. So, I accepted and began to change the focus of my life from Honduras to the world field.

I learned later that Ron had arranged a budget so I could stay in Honduras and continue the program, but by the time I knew this, it was too late to change my mind. Had I known that earlier, I would have been sorely tempted to stay there, for I loved my work in Honduras. Perhaps God knew this and arranged the phone call to come when it did.

Many years later, as I pondered the change, I realized that had I made the decision to go to Fletcher instead of Honduras, I probably would never have been asked to go to the GC. Whether that was good or not, I don't know, but I do know that God's leading in my life was beyond understanding. Even though I was apprehensive about my next assignment, I was grateful to my Shepherd who in Honduras had filled my cup beyond overflowing.

Chapter 17

In Unfamiliar Paths, The GC

Saying goodbye to my good friends in Honduras was difficult, but once the packing was finished and my small shipment was on its way, the time had come. I tearfully said goodbye to Kathy the macaw, who was moving in with the McBrooms. She had been so much fun. Some of my friends took me to the ocean to see it one last time. I ended up with a bright sunburn as a farewell gift from Honduras. My work in Honduras was complete … or so I thought.

Arriving at the airport in the Washington area, the GC driver met me and took me to a GC guest apartment. No! It couldn't be! But it was. They assigned me to the very same apartment where Dick, baby Richie, and I had lived while Dick was taking his master's degree. So many memories flooded back into my mind. The sense of my loss almost overwhelmed me. That first night was difficult.

The next day came culture shock. I had been working in rural Honduras with uneducated people for the most part, struggling with a foreign language, and relating to people who lived at a subsistence level. Now my position required me to relate to highly educated people in a city environment. Uncle Duane (my mother's brother) was now an associate secretary of the GC and Aunt Shirley was registrar for Home Study Institute. They were my angels in a time of need. I arranged for an apartment so my belongings had a place to land, and in a few days, I was on the plane again, this time headed to Campion Academy for Carmen's graduation.

What a special time graduation was. Carmen had done well both scholastically and socially. She had made many friends, and once again she was saying good-bye with tears. After I sold our single-wide home, we tucked in a fun few days of camping with Rosy—first in the Sand Dunes and then in another campground at a higher altitude. In the morning when we woke, the alpine meadow surrounding our tent was not only blanketed with snow but also alive with mountain bluebirds. Their songs provided a glorious goodbye to Colorado.

Arriving back in Takoma Park, my uncle informed me that the apartment that I had chosen was too dangerous, and he had rented a different one for me. He kindly placed the things we had shipped from Honduras in the new apartment. The previous occupants hadn't wanted to take their furniture, so I purchased it from them. What a blessing it was to have the furniture all provided rather than to spend time shopping for it.

Uncle Duane and Aunt Shirley planned on retiring that year. Not knowing how long it would take to sell their house, they listed it early. To their surprise, it sold almost immediately, so they moved in with me for the remainder of the year. What a serendipity!

How my life changed. Now it was to the office, not to the mountains. To dress up every day was a challenge, and it required that I invest in a whole new wardrobe. Joining the staff at the GC was a major adjustment. There was no orientation. It was expected that persons in that position had been working in the conference, union, or division offices, and already knew the ropes. From Elder Baasch and Uncle Duane, I gradually learned many of particulars and policies I needed to know.

Dr. Ruth White, my immediate predecessor, had already set up my itinerary for several months ahead. The first item was a trip to Israel for a nurses meeting in the Euro-Africa Division. This was to happen almost immediately. Since I was totally unprepared, it seemed best to cancel that trip.

The next trip she had arranged was with the Inter-American Division to hold seminars on nursing leadership at several hospitals. Grace Scheresky, vice president for nursing at Hinsdale, consented to co-teach the seminars with me. This seemed more manageable.

On the Island of Curacao, we received a rude awakening to the realities of traveling for the GC. The president of the church in Curacao showed us around the island on Friday, then said, "Oh, and by the way, we are having an island-wide meeting on health tomorrow and plan on you being the speakers." Really? With no forewarning? Grace and I put our heads together that evening and came up with a profitable message.

A different kind of experience awaited us in Honduras. I expected Honduras to be one of my easiest assignments because I considered it my home turf. I knew the place, I knew the people, and I could speak the language. Nurses came from Mexico, and from other places in the Central American Union to the Hospital Adventista de Honduras. We had a good week together, and on Friday evening Grace and I relaxed at the McBroom's home. It was good to be back with Kathy, the macaw. Grace was tired, and she soon left to go to a guest room near the hospital. JoAnn and I talked until late, but I eventually went upstairs to my room. JoAnn and Ron went down to their room just off the dining room.

I was almost ready to crawl into bed when there was a loud crash. What could be going on? Before I had time to react, the ominous sound of heavy boots came stomping up the spiral staircase. Soon there was an insistent knock on my door. I opened it and there stood a masked man with a gun in each hand.

"Donde esta su esposo?" (Where is your husband?)

I replied, "I don't have a husband."

"Come with me," he ordered.

Upstairs in the house I was staying at, there were three bedrooms and a bath. He led us to the next door and commanded me to knock. This was Ronda's room, the teenage daughter of the McBroom's. My heart sank as I lifted my hand to knock. I thought, 'How frightening this will be for Ronda!' Then I remembered she had gone to spend the evening with friends, and was to be back at 10:00 p.m. It was now after 10, but she had not returned. The door opened on an empty room. How fortunate!

Then it was on to the next door. A new doctor, Dr. Orozco, was using this room. I knocked, and he came to the door, only to be told to come with the masked man. He led us both down the winding stairway and what a sight met our eyes. Beside the table in the dining room was a large window. This had been broken and splinters of glass covered the table, the floor, and had gone on into the kitchen. Drops of blood added to the sinister scene. (The blood was from one of the masked men who had cut his hand climbing in the window.) Across the dining room stood another gunman with his gun pointed at Ron standing by his bedroom door. The gunman indicated that all of us should go into the bedroom. Here I was barefooted. How could I walk across the splintered glass? On the counter were all of my travel documents. He reached over with his gun and scattered these on the floor so I could walk on them.

Now they had all of us in the bedroom. JoAnn was sitting on the bed with a sheet pulled around her. They instructed Ron to get dressed and to go with them. They wanted money from the hospital, but Ron told them there was not that kind of money in the business office. The men then gave Dr. Orozco a note and stated there would be dire consequences if anyone contacted the police. They put Ron into the hospital vehicle parked at the house and took off for Tegucigalpa.

Before we had time to react, Ronda returned home. (She had providentially been delayed because she had been helping in the emergency room at the hospital.) When she entered the doorway of their home, she was horrified at the sight of glass and blood. She asked, "What is going on?" JoAnn informed Ronda that her dad had been kidnapped. The hospital vehicle had met her as she was coming home, but she had no idea what was happening. One of the kidnappers asked the other kidnapper whether or not they should stop and get the girl. He replied, "I don't think so." Later we found out that originally Ronda had been the intended victim.

Dr. Orozco then got on the CB radio we used (phone lines were not available at the hospital yet) and asked Dr. Frank McNiel to come to the house immediately. Of course, he responded quickly.

We felt so helpless. What should we do? And that note, what did it say? Dr. Orozco shared the contents: "This is a kidnapping. If you let the authorities or the news media know, we will kill him and dissect him, a fate that will befall each of you, Yankees, invaders of the hospital. If you do not comply with our petitions, our organization does not pardon. The people are with us, and the victory will be ours. "LIVE THE REVOLUTION. DEATH TO YANKEE IMPERIALISM." We decided that before we took any action, we should disperse and get dressed (we had been ready for bed), then meet in the living room to decide what to do next.

As I was dressing, I heard a new noise. It sounded like drawers being opened and shut. Once again, I heard voices.

After being kidnapped, Ron had been praying and thinking rapidly. How should he respond? Recently, he had read an article in an old magazine on how to react if kidnappers came to your home. The advice given was to delay them as much as possible and upset their schedule. Yes, he might be able to do that.

As the kidnappers were driving past the hospital, Ron mentioned that the car might not have enough gas to get to Tegucigalpa. The driver chose to drive on without getting gas. They had not gone far when the motor sputtered and died. The gunmen decided to walk Ron back to the hospital to get a can of gas at the shop gas pumps. On the road they took off their masks to avoid suspicion.

As they approached the hospital, Ron said he would need to go to his office to get the key. He thought he could possibly slip through the Emergency Room door and slam it shut behind him. The gunmen were slipping their masks on as he unlocked the door. Unfortunately, one of them stuck a foot in the door. Ron tried to run across the Emergency Room to the other door, but was grabbed,and a pistol was stuck in his back. Armando, one of the lab technicians who had been talking with the nurses on the unit, heard the noise. Thinking there was another emergency, he came to see what was going on. They took him hostage also.

The kidnappers now decided they would return to Ron's house and get the old Chevy Blazer that was parked there. Ron knew the key for the Blazer was in the ignition, so as he slid into the passenger seat, he hooked it with his finger and pushed it under the seat. Ron told them there were some keys on his dresser, so one of them came and asked JoAnn to find the key for it. The noise I had heard was JoAnn searching for the key. As hospital administrator, Ron always had a bunch of keys on his dresser, so JoAnn gave the kidnapper a handful of keys. When they couldn't find any that worked, they brought Ron and Armando into the house and gathered us all in the bedroom again.

I thought, "Where is Ronda? Where is Frank?" The answer was that Frank had heard Ron and the kidnappers walking up the gravel road, so he took Ronda out the back door and told her to hide behind some potted plants, so they would not kidnap her as well. Frank scooted up to the outside balcony and flattened himself on the balcony just a few feet above where the Blazer was parked.

With all of us in control under their guns, Ron now suggested they send Armando back to the hospital to get the hospital vehicle they used as ambulance. It always had gas, and a key was kept at the nursing unit. He soon came back ashen-faced without the ambulance and explained that he couldn't find the key. Ron sent Armando back with the shop key, as well as the key for the key-cabinet inside the shop. At last, Armando returned with the ambulance.

While Armando was getting the vehicle, we waited, held in the bedroom with the guns pointed at us. Would they kill us? Strangely, I had no fear of death, but only thought of my poor family being faced with another tragedy. Evidently to escape this scene, I had an out-of-body experience. It was like I was not really part of what was going on. I was somewhere in the distance just watching it.

Finally, Armando returned with the correct key, and Ron and the gunmen left again, leaving the house feeling very empty.

Frank and Ronda came back into the house. We discussed what to do next. The local police only had a crank type phone. It was not practical to go there. Asking for God's guidance, Frank decided to drive to the home of a friend who was working in the United States embassy in Tegucigalpa, notify them of what happened, and to get their advice. The rest of us met for a session of prayer. No one panicked or became hysterical. We trusted in the Lord to handle the situation, but it was a long, stressful night. We all wondered what was happening to Ron.

In the morning JoAnn and I decided to go to McNiel's house and help their two children, a boy and a girl, get some breakfast and get ready for Sabbath School. Dr. Janet had been away for some time waiting to deliver a baby. We were going in the door when the dog began to bark. We turned to see why. Could it be? Were we seeing what we thought our eyes were telling us? Ron was coming up the steps! What a joyous reunion!

Ron briefly told us that he had been taken to an apartment in Tegucigalpa but had been released. He needed to pick up his check book and other items and go back to Tegucigalpa. Ron learned that Frank had been to the home of the embassy person, had come back to the hospital to get a variety of items, and had returned. Ron picked up what he needed and left again, this time to meet Frank.

With many questions in our minds, we helped the children prepare for the day and went to Sabbath School with them. The men returned at noon and told their story.

Ron had been told to lie on the bed in the apartment bedroom, and the kidnapper kept guard outside the room. The other men left. Ron heard shots and a commotion outside, but he had no idea what was happening. Then all was quiet. Ron asked his guard if they could talk. The answer was, "No." Again and again Ron asked, but he was rebuffed each time. Finally, at about 4 a.m. the kidnapper came to the door and said, "What do you want to talk about?"

Ron asked, "Why am I being kidnapped?"

The kidnapper had been indoctrinated into communist thought and replied, "We are fighting for a better life for the people, and the "gringos" are taking advantage of the people."

Ron said, "So are we, only we do it by taking care of people's health needs." He gave a little history of the hospital and how we helped the people of the village. Ron then asked if he could pray for both of them. He prayed a simple prayer. The kidnapper closed the bedroom door, and things were quiet again.

Finally, the kidnapper came to the door once more. This time he said, "I know you don't deserve to be kidnapped. However, if I don't give them what they want, they will probably kill me. If I let you escape, my leader will kill me. I must leave the country, but I have no money."

Ron kept the kidnapper talking, and together they came up with a plan. If Ron would give him enough money to buy a plane ticket to Panama, he would let him go. They agreed to meet at noon the next day in the central plaza, and Ron would give him the money. Ron was to put the money in a folded newspaper, get his shoes shined at the shoe shine stand, and leave the paper as he left. With this agreement, the kidnapper gave Ron the camera he had stolen at the house and enough money for bus fare back to the hospital. They walked out of the apartment and went their separate ways.

When Ron went back to Tegucigalpa to find Frank, Ron found Frank talking with a policeman. The policeman was able to tell him about the shots he had heard in the night: The second kidnapper had gone to the National Department of Police Investigation (like the "FBI") and called from the corner to the guard on duty in front of the office saying he needed help. When the guard got to the corner, the kidnapper whipped out a pistol and shot the guard twice, grabbed his rifle, and ran. (The guard later recovered.) Two agents on duty inside the office heard the shots and gave chase. There was a running gun battle. They caught up with the kidnapper as he was trying to open the apartment door. He was shot and killed. They kept the building under surveillance the remainder of the night, then at about 5 a.m. left for a little while to get reinforcements. It was during this time that Ron and his kidnapper left. Once the reinforcements got to the apartment complex, the building was searched. They found a bomb ready to go off when two wires were joined. What would have happened if they had searched the building when Ron was inside?

Ron told the policeman about his agreement with the kidnapper. The police insisted that he keep his appointment, and the police would capture the kidnapper when he picked up the newspaper. Ron was sorry he had to do this, as he felt the young man had been touched by the Lord that night, and he would be letting the young man down. Nevertheless, Ron went to the bank at the appointed time. Whoops, the bank was closed. He had never been to the bank on a Sabbath morning and did not know the bank was closed then. Now what? He went to the park, sat on a bench in front of the church and wrote a note to the kidnapper saying why he could not cash the check. As he finished writing, someone sat down beside him. It was the kidnapper! They talked a few minutes. Ron gave him the note and check, and they parted. Not one policeman had seen him!

Ron came back to the hospital with two bodyguards. Later he went to the vehicle that ran out of gas and was left by the road. When he turned the key, it started up immediately. He drove it several miles before needing to switch to the spare tank.

We thanked God for answering our prayers. All of us were safe.

The next morning Grace and I left for the states, grateful that the incident had been resolved so quickly.

The newspaper reported that the kidnapper was caught on Monday morning when he was trying to cash the check at the bank. The account stated that he was showing the police a hideout where their group had a store of weapons and while trying to escape, he was shot and killed. Two others involved in the plot were imprisoned.

Part of my sadness over this incident was the fact that our kidnappers were young university students who had made some wrong decisions and had been snared by the communists to the loss of their lives. The communists had targeted students who were struggling with their studies. They had invited them to evening study sessions where they promised help with difficult subjects. The communists helped them with the subjects, true, but at the same time, they indoctrinated them with communism.

As I reviewed the incident, I remembered the many times I had hiked alone over the very same territory with never a thought about my personal safety. The implications shocked me. Had I been in danger for those three years? If so, how many times had God protected me in my innocence?

Five years later I returned to Honduras with a team doing hospital surveys. I found that the Adventist Church had spawned several new churches within ten miles from the mother church. When the hospital work had started, there were no Adventists in the area. I was amazed at what God had wrought!

Chapter 18

His Sheep Know His Voice, London

My travel papers were in place, my ticket was in hand, and my teaching materials were prepared. I thought I was ready for my trip to the Trans Africa Division. Then the day before flight time, I thought of the immunizations I needed. I checked my records, and yes, I should have several. Horrors! The only thing to do was get those shots that same day. I also began taking chloroquin to prevent malaria.

The following evening the GC driver took me to Dulles Airport, and I boarded a British Airways Boeing 747 bound for London. After the overnight flight, there was an all-day wait in London until I could board the next flight bound to Nairobi, Kenya.

I was tired from lack of sleep, ill from the immunizations, and feeling lousy from the chloroquin. The old devil recognized my time of weakness. Always the coward, Satan saw this was a good time to assail me with doubts. Why did this Iowa farm girl think anything good could be accomplished by her going to Africa? He offered many reasons why I should not be doing this: I was not qualified. I might get sick. I might encounter poisonous snakes. I didn't know the culture. I didn't know the languages. They wouldn't listen to a mere woman. It was useless to go. Traveling alone was lonesome … On and on he concocted objections.

In that crowded, noisy airport, I sat and prayed, "Lord, why did you ask me to do this? What do you want of me in Africa?"

Then I thought through my situation. Yes, Phyllis Collins, the division nurse, was driving up to Blantye, Malawi from Lesotho to meet me. We were to hold nursing leadership seminars in the various hospitals on our way back to Lesotho. I had prepared my subject material, but surely God must have a greater reason for my going.

Finally, after some time, I decided to ask God for three things, plus a fourth: (1) For eyes to recognize the needs I could address; (2) For protection on my travels; (3) For the ability to do whatever I was asked (after the Curacao experience, I had learned that this could be anything, and only God could give me words to speak at the last minute); plus, (4) To always represent Him correctly.

High up on the wall in the London airport, there was a board that lists the incoming and outgoing flights. In my mental fog, I watched as the letters and numbers kept flipping down the board giving new flight information. Hour after hour the flight numbers, destinations, arrival times, and departure times scrolled on and on. Finally, finally, the flight to Nairobi was listed on the "flipping" board, and I was on my way.

As my plane approached Nairobi the following morning, dawn broke. From my seat by the window, the Lord gave me a special promise in the sky. It wasn't a Noah-rainbow. It wasn't an eclipse or a falling star. It was a glorious, spectacular cloud extravaganza that completely encircled the plane. Above me the shimmering clouds were a kaleidoscope of red, as was the mist below. It looked like Africa was on fire. As I gazed in wonder, I felt God was speaking specifically to me in a language I could understand. This was His cloud. This was God's way of telling me that He had accepted my requests and that He was promising to grant my heart's plea. In my soul I knew God was with me.

After another wait, I was on the plane to Blantyre and to my introduction to Africa.

CHAPTER 19

Faithful Shepherd, First Promise Fulfilled

God answered my first request of Him, "For eyes to recognize the needs that I could address," in at least three ways: (1) By seeing the need for another School of Nursing in Africa; (2) By identifying a need in health education which could be met; and (3) By making me aware of the need for Spiritual Care Seminars.

Another School Of Nursing

It was a pleasure to work with Phyllis Collins and get acquainted with this capable, dedicated lady who had years of experience in Africa. As we visited the hospitals, I was stunned. In the Inter-American and South American Divisions, with which I was well acquainted, the hospitals were staffed with qualified national nurses. The first missionaries to those divisions had made education a high priority, and they had created several nursing schools. But this was not true in Africa.

In Africa, I found the hospitals were largely staffed with overseas missionary nurses, as were some of the clinics. There were several Seventh-day Adventist nursing schools in Africa that provided training somewhat equivalent to a licensed vocational nurse (LVN) or licensed practical nurse (LPN) degree, except they also included courses for mid-wife certification. There was one RN (registered nurse) nursing school at Maluti Hospital in Lesotho. (Lesotho is a small country surrounded by South Africa.) Before the spread of communism, there had been another nursing school in Addis Ababa, Ethiopia, but that had been closed. Considering that Africa is a huge continent with many Adventist hospitals and clinics, surely there was a need for many more schools of nursing, especially at the RN and bachelor's levels.

As we traveled, Phyllis and I began to dream—not only of creating another Adventist

RN nursing school, but also of an Adventist BS nursing school. (There were RN and BS nursing programs in the South African public system, but nowhere else that we knew.) How could we make this happen? We began by talking with Dr. Handysides, the division health and temperance director over Africa. He had been supportive of Phyllis' plan to assist graduates from Maluti Hospital in Lesotho in obtaining a bachelor's degree by correspondence from the University of South Africa. Yes, Dr. Handysides heartily supported our concept of opening a BS school of nursing, and he put it on committee agendas to begin the process.

The idea raised a multitude of questions. Where should such a school be located? Who would finance it? What should the curriculum include? What about faculty? Should this school be at one of the hospitals? Or, should it be at located at a college/university? It seemed to us that it would be difficult to accomplish without being placed in a college/university setting. Adventist higher-level education for much of Africa was still in its infancy. What college might fit our needs? Solusi College (in Zimbabwe) had been started some years before, but could not yet grant government-recognized degrees. (This has since changed.) A university was being developed in Kenya and another in Rwanda. We began to focus on Kenya since there had never been a BS school of nursing there.

We traveled and dreamed and considered some of the obstacles to such a venture. At Heri Hospital in Tanzania, I met a young nurse who impressed me as a possibility of becoming a faculty member if she could obtain adequate education. I presented this possibility to the Association of Seventh-day Adventist Nurses for Sponsorship. They voted to help her go to the Philippines to earn her bachelor's degree. She was delighted with this opportunity. Eventually, she did come back and serve on the faculty of our new school.

Before I finished my work at the GC, in 1988, the BS school of nursing became a reality on the campus of the University of East Africa in Kenya. This was because of the local work of Phyllis Collins and Dr. Handysides, and me meeting with many committees, both in Africa and at the GC.

By the time this actually happened, Phyllis had moved on to other responsibilities. Sosamma Lindsay, a nurse from India, became the first teacher/chairperson of the nursing school. She faced many challenges, one of these being the fact that the hospitals in Kenya expected the nursing school to pay fees to the nearby hospitals for the privilege of allowing their students to practice nursing there. Besides that, the students had to bring their own equipment to give patient care, including bedpans, urinals, wash basins, etc. Another challenge was the level of care available in the hospitals. It did not reach the standard that Sosamma wished to reach for her students. The challenges were faced and resolved one by one.

This school has prospered, and last I heard, it was dialoguing with Loma Linda University to begin a master's program in nursing. The university has also collaborated with Loma Linda to offer an MPH (Masters of Public Health). This development is gratifying to me. The results are well worth the many hours I spent in committees.

Health Education

In addition to nursing education, I was concerned about health education for the general population in developing countries. The need for the knowledge of basic hygiene was obvious everywhere we went.

On a later trip to the Africa-Indian Ocean Division, I traveled with Dr. Barry Wecker, the health and temperance director for that division. He also had an interest in public health education. We tossed about possibilities of how we might make a positive difference, and we came up with the idea of creating a "health educator" position in each local church (like churches have religious liberty secretaries and stewardship secretaries). We realized, however, that these health educators would need training and tools to do their work. Over time, the idea of co-authoring a book took shape, and we began working toward that goal. This was a challenge because we were living on different continents. After much work by us and the editor, *The Church Health Educator* was published by MacMillan Publishers in 1989. This was a book written specifically for Africa.

Publishing the book was the first step. The second step was training the health educators and introducing this book. Dr. Wecker and I made a trip to the hospitals and universities of his division co-teaching classes based on the book. Some of the attendees were nurses, but more often they were pastors. They especially thanked us for giving them some very practical information.

The concept needed much broader exposure in the other divisions, but personnel and division lines changed, and this did not happen. As I looked back on it later, I realized what I should have done. I should have contacted various other denominations in Africa and introduced the concept of church health educators to them and offered the book as a tool. But at that point, I was accustomed to the protocol of being invited to a division for a specific purpose, and it did not occur to me to travel to different countries in Africa without division sponsorship to make contact with the other denominations. Would it have been successful? Having not tried it, I will never know. The book is still being used, but it could have had a much wider impact. When all the books were sold, it was not republished as far as I know.

Spiritual Care Seminars

As I traveled around Africa, it surprised me how many missionary wives and single missionary ladies confided in me. The representatives from the GC that usually came through were almost entirely men, and the women missionaries did not feel comfortable sharing their troubles with them. I spent considerable time listening to them. I was a safe person to whom they could unburden themselves because I was soon leaving their campus, and their tales would go no further than my ears and heart. Having spent time as a missionary myself, I could identify with their situations.

This opened my eyes to a need for developing spiritual care seminars. As I prepared the seminar materials, it seemed the Holy Spirit was by my side making suggestions. These were presented mostly in Africa because that is where we had the most missionaries, but it was also used in other places. Many people told me that these seminars had been extremely helpful to them personally and professionally.

Also, as far as possible, I would send each of the overseas missionary nurses a birthday card each year. Many of them told me how much they appreciated that.

Indeed, in Africa and beyond, my Faithful Shepherd answered my prayer "For eyes to recognize the needs that I could address." He also provided practical solutions to meet those needs.

Chapter 20

Faithful Shepherd, Second Promise Fulfilled

As before, God was faithful in fulfilling my second request for "Protection on my travels." How? Two incidents illustrate this:

A Leaky Gas Tank

Once again I took that long flight to Malawi. This time, Phyllis, Marilyn Bennett, and Dudu Majola met me at the airport. (Phyllis and I made three trips together—two by car and one by plane.) On this trip we held a series of seminars. Early on, she warned me that we might experience a potentially serious problem that could complicate our trip.

Phyllis had sponsored a boy through school. She was in the States on furlough when this student had vacation. In Africa, not only do you help students in school, but when you do, they consider you their parent. When he came for vacation to Maluti Hospital, he stayed in Phyllis' home even though she was in the United States. As is typical of students, he wanted some diversion. He looked around and found the key to her car. Yes, that was just the thing he needed for a little excitement! He would go for a ride. Had he had driven before? No, but he had watched others drive. Certainly it could not be too difficult, so off he went. I'm sure it was fun until he ended up on a pile of rocks, seriously damaging the underside of her car.

When Phyllis returned, she faced the problem of getting her car repaired. She took it to a garage in the nearest town in South Africa and stressed to the mechanics the necessity of getting the car repaired quickly. She explained that she was scheduled to leave on a long trip to Malawi, and it was urgent that it be repaired. She must begin traveling soon, or there would not be adequate time to meet me in Malawi. The mechanics did their best. Everything was repaired, except the gas tank. The replacement one had not yet arrived. The mechanics assured her the damage was high up on the tank, and if she did not fill the tank to the top, there should not be a problem. So, she began the trip with her friends.

The mechanics were correct for a while. We made it to Malamulo Hospital in Malawi, then went on to Mwami Hospital in Zambia, holding seminars at each place. Because of political problems, Phyllis thought it wise not to go through Zimbabwe. Instead, she chose to go through Zambia to Victoria Falls and down the length of Botswana to Kanye Hospital. We drove on to Lusaka to spend the night and left early the next morning. Some distance out of Lusaka, we stopped at a lay-by to eat breakfast. Someone happened to notice that gas ("petrol" in Africa) was dripping from the gas tank. Oh no! Gas in Zambia was about $5.00 a liter (a quart). It was like dripping gold onto the road, and there was no help available. There would be no way of fixing it in Lusaka; gas stations were few and far between.

I had heard of people solving the problem with chewing gum. Did we have any? Incredibly, we did. Before leaving Lesotho, one of the ladies had thought she might want to chew gum along the trip and had purchased a supply. It had not yet been chewed. So, we busily chewed gum, and Phyllis plugged the hole. It worked! With the leak taken care of for the moment, we traveled on our way, praying that God would provide for our needs. Every once in a while, Phyllis would stop and hang her head down under the car so she could see the gas tank. When it began to leak again, we chewed more gum. Unfortunately, this was sugarless gum and dissolved more readily than other kinds of gum.

After while Phyllis said, "There is an Adventist boarding school here somewhere. I don't know how far it is off the main highway, but perhaps if we can get there, they can help us."

At last we saw the sign to the Rusongu Secondary School and turned down a sandy road. We had not gone far when we met a pickup. A classmate of Phyllis' from academy days was driving it! He informed us that the principal of the school, A. W. Spaulding, had driven logging trucks and was very knowledgeable about mechanics. We should go see him. He indicated that the school was not far down the road, so we quickly made our way there.

It was true; the principal was very helpful. He told us it would be impossible to solder the crack that was causing the leak because the tank would explode, but there was something else we could do. We could use soft soap. He said it worked better than gum. He gave us some soap, which Phyllis applied. After that, we were on our way to Victoria Falls and then to Botswana. That soap held all the way to Kanye hospital where it finally began leaking again and needed more soap.

After teaching at Kanye hospital, we headed across South Africa toward Lesotho. A major thunder-lightning storm with heavy rain welcomed us to Maluti Hospital, the home of my three companions. We quickly prepared for the Sabbath and were glad to get some rest.

Early the next morning, Phyllis started her car and drove off to Sabbath school. She was still on campus when the car stopped. You guessed it. There was no gas. The rain from the evening before had washed the soap out of the crack, and the gas had leaked out. Back in the mechanic shop the next week, the new gas tank was installed.

Certainly the Lord had blessed us women. He took care of the gas tank until we were safe at home. We praised Him for His watchful care.

The Missed Flight in Lagos

While holding health education seminars, Dr. Wecker and I visited many hospitals and colleges in the Africa-Indian Ocean Division. Our last session was at the Adventist Seminary of West Africa (now Babcock University) in Nigeria. This is some distance from the capital city of Lagos. This seminar had been tailored for the pastors in Nigeria. They expressed appreciation for the information conveyed, and for the book. We enjoyed the interaction with them and with the staff at the seminary.

On our last day there, as we were eating breakfast at the home of the president, I showed my airline ticket to those at the table. We all agreed that I was scheduled to leave the following day. Caleb Adeogun, President of the Nigerian Union, requested I stay at the college until the next day, as accommodations in Lagos were difficult.

When the seminar was over, Dr. Wecker and others left to go to the airport in Lagos. I relaxed for the evening and enjoyed the birds of Nigeria. The next morning the president came to me and said, "Have you heard the news?"

"What news?" I said.

"Your flight was at 12:01 a.m. (midnight), and you should have been at the airport, but I will arrange for someone to take you to Lagos tomorrow, and we will see what we can do." At that time Nigeria's airport was one of the most chaotic airports in all my travels. This could not have happened at a much worse place.

The Bible teacher at the college ended up chauffeuring me to the airport. Along the way, much to my delight, he regaled me with stories of what it was like growing up in a multiple-wife home in Nigeria. He reported that the husband (his father) dare not eat food prepared by any of the wives for fear of being poisoned because they all hated each other so much. Had not the gospel found them, they probably would have killed each other. He expressed his joy at the changes that happened when they became Christians.

He took me to the union office, and that evening Pastor Adeogun took me to the airport to see if he could get me on a plane. The clerks informed us that the plane was full, but if we went in the next room to wait, perhaps some passenger would not show up, and I could get on the plane.

We went into the next room and waited with dozens of other people, all hoping to board the plane. After a while, the person in charge asked us all to leave because all the seats on the plane had been taken.

The following day, Pastor Adeogun took me to various airline offices attempting to arrange a flight. Unsympathetic personnel bluntly told us, "There is no possibility of getting a flight. It will probably be a month before we can get you a seat." Bad news. A helper at the union office took me to a near-by market to purchase a little food.

The next day, a more kindly airline clerk told us to go to the airport that night and try to get on, as we had before. The story was the same. "Go into the next room to wait and see if a seat becomes available." Once again the room was full of hopeful people, and again the attendant told us to all leave.

Then Pastor Adeogun suggested, "Let's just stand to one side until everyone else is gone." So, we waited as the disappointed people left. When the room was quiet, Pastor Adeogun approached the attendant, told him of our plight, and begged him for a seat. The attendant allowed us to go through his door. Before I could leave the country, though, I had to pass several check-points for verification of passports, etc. Finally, we were at the last check-point. Could I really leave? The official told us, "No. There is no room for you on this flight."

Just then Pastor Adeogun spied a very well-dressed African man. He happily went to greet him. This could not be a chance meeting, for I learned he was Pastor Adeogun's brother-in-law who just "happened" to be an ambassador to Ethiopia. The ambassador offered the information that the airlines must always reserve seats for government personnel so they can make last-minute flights if needed. The ambassador showed his passport to the official who had just told me I could not board the plane and muttered a few words. Then the official waved us both on through.

The plane was, indeed, very full, but somehow God found room for me. How thankful I was to be on my way home and not having to wait in Lagos for a month. I believe God arranged for the ambassador to be traveling that very night so he could care for my needs.

Chapter 21

Faithful Shepherd, Third Promise Fulfilled

My third request of God had been, "To give me the ability to do whatever I was asked."

The experience in Curacao was only a small foretaste of the future. The following are brief examples of unexpected tasks I was asked to do at the last moment. There are countless more.

It was not unusual to arrive at a hospital in India and have someone inform me that I was scheduled to speak at the Friday evening meeting, give a mission story for Sabbath School, and take the sermon for the church service. This was a little easier when Liz Sterndale, the North American Division nurse, was with me because she would take half of the appointments, and I would take the other half. Usually, we had at least a couple of hours to think about it, and on that first trip to the Inter-American Division, I had learned to take a few materials with me "just in case." These came in very handy. The Lord also gave us thoughts and illustrations.

On my second trip to India, Liz was not with me. On arriving at our hospital in Ottapalam to give a seminar, the principal of the nearby Adventist school came and asked whether I would be willing to hand out awards on their sports day. They had never had anyone from the GC do this, and it would be an honor for me to do that. The time did not conflict with the seminars, so I agreed. What I anticipated was to hand out awards and shake their hands. When I arrived at the school, though, the principal showed me the program, noting that he expected me to speak to the several hundred students for 10 minutes. Whoops! I did not have that in mind. He ushered me into the faculty lounge where the faculty had gathered. As he opened the door, he said, "We are looking forward to your worship talk this morning." My eyes bulged, and I realized my prayers for help must be quick! Fortunately, by now, I had given a number of worship talks and selected one from my mind. Only a few minutes remained before my part in the sports program, and I rushed another urgent prayer upward. What would I say? I remembered once having given a talk to youth on reaching one's goals in life. That might be appropriate. "God," I pleaded, "bring to my mind enough of that talk to inspire these students." Once again, He came through.

One time while I was in Africa, I arrived at Kendu Bay Hospital in Kenya, and the nursing school instructor came with a new request: Graduation was to be held that evening, would I please give the graduation address? At least this time I had a few hours to think about what I might say to a graduating class. As these experiences took place, I developed talks and materials on a number of topics to always carry with me, but I could not foresee every situation.

Perhaps the most uncomfortable request I could not refuse came in Argentina. The division nurse had arranged, unbeknownst to me, for me to speak to a special meeting of the nurses' association of Argentina. This was a new one. All the materials I would need to put together such a talk were in Washington, D.C. I am afraid that was a time when even the help of the Lord was inadequate. I gave a talk, but not the kind I would have liked to give had I been able to prepare back in the office.

More difficult, perhaps, was to hear and see problems that I had no power to change. In people's personal lives, I could only listen sympathetically. I suspect, though, they did not really expect resolution, only an opportunity to share. The institutional problems were much more difficult. How much of what I saw should I report to colleagues and administration, and how much should I just recognize and record? I probably did not always do this correctly. My position was not one of authority, but one to only give advice and encouragement.

In Rwanda at Mugonero Hospital, the principal of the near-by school asked me to give a worship talk. This was doable, I thought, so at the appointed time, I met with the students and faculty for worship. Interestingly, after worship the principal showed me around the campus and was rather indignant when I did not offer money to sponsor a student. I assured him that my own daughter was in college, and I could not help him with tuition. He finally accepted that (what else could he do?), and I went on my way. I often had the feeling that many institutions were far more interested in receiving financial assistance rather than in receiving the professional and individual advice we offered at our seminars. To their disappointment, we did not have money to distribute.

At Mountain View College in the Philippines, I faced another type of challenge. The student missionaries there went to remote mountain villages to teach and share the gospel. I was asked to visit some of the students who were living in a village so remote that it would take four days to hike there. However, I wouldn't have to walk four days. Instead, I could go there in the college plane, which would leave the next day. (I happened to be staying in the home of the pilot.) Suddenly, I was faced with a decision. Ever since the accident, I had avoided flying in private planes. Would I let this prevent me from a rewarding experience, or would I ask the Lord to help me overcome my fears and go? My decision was to go.

In the village I found the students living in a bamboo hut that had been built high off the ground. Their school was similar but larger. They had constructed a little church of the same materials. Not only were the students teaching the basics of education, but they were also teaching hygiene to the adults. Just bathing in water had greatly decreased many of the skin diseases that usually plagued them. It was a treat to see the dedication of these student missionaries.

It was fortunate that I confronted my fears, for several other times in my travels, it was necessary to go by small plane. One of those times was the third trip I made with Phyllis across Africa.

All-in-all, I felt God fulfilled His promise to enable me to do what I was asked.

As to my fourth request to God, "To always represent Him correctly," only heaven knows how God answered that. Being the faithful God I found Him to be, I rest that with Him.

Chapter 22
His Goodness And Mercy

In addition to doing my work at the GC, I had a personal life.

My father had been ill when I went to the GC, and after a lengthy illness, he passed away. Once again, the family gathered for a funeral. Although we knew Dad was tired of being sick and was tired of living, it still hurt our family. Mom had also been critically ill while he was sick, and it was a miracle she was well enough to attend the funeral. At that occasion we promised ourselves we would have a family reunion that did not involve a funeral. We kept that promise and met together at a park near where MaryEtta lived in South Dakota. Many of the next generation came, and what a wonderful time we had. A special tent was put up, so Mom would be comfortable.

At the GC, there were several of us single ladies who traveled a lot. We would come home to empty refrigerators, and sometimes we had been gone so long that no one even

With the spouses we surround Mom.

While I was still in Honduras, Carmen had decided to go to Union College to study nursing after graduation from Campion. All of her friends were going to Union College. She wished to continue with those plans even though I now lived a few blocks from Columbia Union College. After her first year she accompanied me on a portion of a trip to the Far Eastern Division. These "animals" are in front of our hospital in Taiwan

remembered us socially. I decided to do something about it, so I invited the ladies to my home for a Friday evening soup and Bible study. It gave us opportunity to discuss our needs with each other. We found the evening most satisfying. All around we were asking, "Could we get together on a regular basis? Perhaps we might rotate homes?" Everyone agreed this was a good idea, and so, we often met together, each lady finding the support and friendship she craved. After returning from one rather lengthy trip, I learned that the group had decided it would be better to meet on Saturday nights. Some had observed that people who live alone do not laugh enough. By meeting on Saturday nights, we could play games, be silly, and laugh. I smile just thinking about how much fun we had together.

Carmen and I agreed that I would come to Union College for Thanksgivings, and we would drive to Iowa to see my mother. This worked well because Bob, Grace's husband, had helped me buy a car for Carmen for her academy graduation (she was to get the title when she graduated from college), so we had transportation. We enjoyed the trips to Iowa each year. When we arrived in Ruthven, we bundled Mom into the car and drove on up to MaryEtta's house in South Dakota to be with the rest of the family. MaryEtta had six children, so with spouses and grandchildren, it made a large, fun, group. Each year, it snowed and made travel difficult, but every time we were kept safe. We thanked the Lord for watching over us on the treacherous roads.

Then came that very special weekend when Carmen and her boyfriend, Evert, along with several of her second cousins graduated from Union College. Again there were many tears of goodbye, and the usual concerns of what the future held. (By the way, she did get the title to her car.) Carmen and Evert both chose to come to Takoma Park and live near their parents. (Evert's father was the pastor of the Pennsylvania Avenue church in Washington, D.C.) Carmen was studying for state boards, which she took in Baltimore. Those were anxious days for her. At last, she was a registered nurse and worked in labor and delivery.

Now a college graduate and professional nurse.

One time after being out of my office for a few days attending meetings at Andrews, I returned to find a note on my desk requesting me to phone Al Stober. I remembered Al as a member of the Kirkland church in Washington State. Why would he want me to call? Did he want me to come and assist with some health education in the church in Kirkland, Washington? The pastor of the Kirkland had mentioned that possibility to me. Perhaps Al was following up that contact on behalf of the pastor? If so, this would be easy to handle, for North America was the responsibility of Liz Sterndale, so, I would simply direct his request to her for her to handle when she returned to her office.

Somehow, I couldn't dismiss the note easily. I reached back into my memory. What did I remember about Al? Very little. He and his family (wife and two children) were members of the Kirkland church when I was there. I remembered that he taught a Sabbath School class, although not the one I attended. His wife had stayed in the background, so I had never gotten acquainted with her. Still puzzled, I phoned Al.

Al informed me that life had changed for his family. His wife had developed cancer. At first the treatments seemed successful, but, eventually, the cancer returned and took her life. Now he was looking for a new relationship. Could we become acquainted? Wow! This was totally unexpected. The possibility of remarriage had seemed remote. None of the single men I had met over the years had appealed to me. How should I respond? What would God want me to do? I told him I would have to think about this. After a good while, I consented to correspond.

How does one form a relationship with someone on the other side of continent at my age? After corresponding awhile, I decided that since I had been single now for 15 years and had grown accustomed to making my own decisions, it was best to forget this relationship.

If a suitable relationship had been offered years earlier, I would have been more tempted. Only one who is a widow understands what it is like to be single, especially one who is a single parent. Most social activities, especially in the church, are planned for families, not for singles. After Dick died, most of our couple friends were no longer comfortable including me without my family. This was distressing for them as well as for me, as they really didn't know what to say or do. My sister, who was divorced, said that only women who were very confident in the love of their husbands can allow a single lady to be close to the family. That idea may be a bit extreme, but it carried a grain of truth. Curiously, even sermons on marriage were painful to me. However, by the time Al contacted me, I was comfortable with my single life. In fact, thoughts of remarriage were planets away from my deepest considerations.

In spite of my bent to staying single, the Lord impressed me that it was His plan for me to remarry, that He could handle my deficiencies, and He would put love in my heart for Al.

Before we seriously discussed marriage, I made a visit to Washington State where my sister, Shirley, was food service director of Walla Walla College. Al and I spent a weekend at her home, which offered an opportunity to discuss many aspects of marriage to see whether we would be compatible or not. We finally both decided that yes, we would get married.

After our engagement I told my secretary. Like wildfire, the news spread throughout the department. No one had any idea that I had been communicating with Al, with the exception of Liz and the group of friends with whom I played games with on Saturday nights. (I had told them what was happening the Saturday night before I went to Washington.) Getting over the shock, they quickly pulled together a party in the meeting room. Al moved to Washington, D.C., found a job, and lived at Mattison's in exchange for painting most of the inside of their house.

Once he moved, Al and I began to discuss when we could get married. This was a complicated question, as my travel schedule for the year was already made. We found a spot in the schedule, and the next thing to figure out was what kind of wedding we would have. If it was a large wedding, it could be very large, for there was no way I could limit the list of invitees either from the Burnt Mills church where I attended or from among my many GC friends. We could also have a large family gathering, but that would be complicated. Besides, my family might rather come for Carmen's wedding. We decided to have a small wedding at the home of Reggie and Ellen Mattison. Don Gilbert, GC treasurer officiated. His wife, Irene, had been an academy classmate of mine. Carmen and Evert stood up with us. Aside from those mentioned Evert's parents and the Saturday night group attended.

Our wedding pictures were not the best, this is a later picture.

This was another example of how seemingly small decisions affected my life in unexpected ways. If I had not years before decided to enroll at the University of Washington, then chose to live in Kirkland, Al would have known nothing about me. When I became Iris Stober once again, I was a wife and a mother of three children—Carmen, plus Al's son Doug and daughter Dyvonne, now both grown. God's goodness and mercy had followed me and had eventually come to find me. It felt good, very good.

After a honeymoon trip to Florida, Al settled into my home in Takoma Park, and I headed off overseas. Some of the secretaries at the GC asked me whether I was going to resign now that I was married. My response was, "There are many men in the GC who are married, and I don't see any of them leaving the GC for that reason." That response startled them, but the question revealed to me how far we still had to go in our thinking about the equality of the sexes in the workplace.

Dyvonne

The next big occasion that brought many of the family members together was the wedding of Carmen and Evert. On the day of that wedding, Evert arrived in a vintage Packard. It was fun to be together again for that happy occasion. After their honeymoon, the newlyweds set up housekeeping in a condominium nearby.

Over the next five years, I made three major trips overseas each year. In the spring of 1990, I visited all the hospitals in India and Nepal. The last stop on that long trip was to the hospital in Banepa, a few miles from

Katmandu. The visit was profitable. Soon it was time to move on. An evening flight landed me in the New Delhi airport about midnight. The flight to the States did not leave until morning. As I sat in the airport that night, I thought of the endless hours of sitting in the airports I had done over the last nine years. At times, planes did not fly when they were scheduled. Other times airline schedules had changed, unbeknownst to me. I always worried whether or not the luggage I needed had arrived at my destination. While fascinated with the view of the world church, I was tired, so tired, of traveling.

I remembered Uncle Duane's advice to me when I first went to the GC. He advised me that ten years at the GC were enough (although he did not follow his own advice). Now this was the year of another GC session, a decision time. Arriving back at the GC, I told my boss, Dr. Gordon Hadley, that I did not wish my name to be considered for another term. He convinced me that resigning would not be wise, and I should wait.

Al's son Doug with future wife Kim.

Before the upcoming GC session in Indianapolis, there was considerable discussion about cutting back on staff. Of course, this undercurrent made everyone uneasy about who would be reelected, and who would not. In Indianapolis, this uneasiness proved to be well-grounded, as some were not reelected, including Dr. Hadley. My job was eliminated. Dr. Hadley's advice had been wise. If I had resigned, I would have had minimal benefits. Now I was part of the group who was not reelected, and whoever hired us would benefit from the GC paying our moving expenses and the first six months of salary.

Again I could see God's leading. Seeing that I was ready for a change, and that the Church's needs had changed, it was clear that my GC work was finished. I felt a certain satisfaction and relief at having completed my given task. This time I wasn't worried about the future. My Lord had cared for me thus far, and I was confident He wouldn't abandon me now.

Over the years my traveling itineraries had been planned solely with the object of fulfilling my work responsibilities, not to see the world. Occasionally, though, along the path of duty I was privileged to visit special places and experience unexpected

Carmen and Evert, now happily, Mr. and Mrs. McDowell.

blessings. Here I want to express gratitude for some of these marvelous gifts that God bestowed on me and to react to my experiences over the past nine years at the GC. After all, the Good Book says, "Be thankful unto him, and bless his name. For the LORD is good; his mercy is everlasting" (Ps. 100:4-5 KJV).

Special Blessings

It was a privilege getting acquainted with the GC staff, the missionaries, and the nationals I met around the world. What a dedicated, committed, group of Christians they were. They shared many inspiring stories with me.

God challenged me to my limits at times, but through it all, He met my needs.

Committees seemed endless. Sometimes I wondered whether anyone in the world would know the difference if we scrapped them; but then again, there were committees that led to results of profound importance. I had the opportunity to sit on the Loma Linda Hospital Board and be a part of some tough, challenging decisions. I was thankful that, at least sometimes, God allowed me to see good come out of the apparent drudgery.

Then there was the politics. The reality is: church politics exist at all levels. Through all this intrigue, I have seen that God still continues to lead His church. He is big enough.

Cultures are fascinating, but adapting my teaching to each culture was a challenge. I learned there are many ways to do the same thing, and I learned to say to myself, "Don't be too dogmatic, Iris."

Through all the travel and demands required by this job, I was never seriously ill. In fact, since the accident, neither Carmen nor I experienced any major illnesses. This was particularly significant to me since I had read the results of an extensive study conducted by Thomas H. Holmes and Richard H. Rahe at the University of Washington on the reaction of the body to stress. The study listed various stressors such as a new job, move, divorce, death in the family, birth of a child, etc. and assigned values to each one. Those who scored over a certain number had a high probability of acquiring a serious illness within a relatively short time. Carmen and I both scored way over the top. It was then that I recognized that God had truly blessed us both with good health.

The occasional "tourist" activities were a special privilege. Some of the highlights for me were:

- To visit the Pergamon museum in what was then East Berlin, and to view the cobalt and golden walls of Nebuchadnezzar's Babylon, along with the gate of Ishtar. They were beautiful.
- To visit Germany before and after the wall came down.
- To visit the Taj Majal.
- To visit a number of game parks, especially in Zambia. At each visit the nurses at

Mwami Hospital arranged a day at the game park for them, as well as for us.
- To sit near the mountain gorillas in Rwanda.
- To visit Iguassu and Victoria Falls.
- To see many beautiful birds. I love birds, so early in the mornings I would take the opportunity to watch the birds of the area. It was frustrating at times, though, to take so long to identify them when there were so many new ones.

I am so thankful that God has been good and merciful to me.

Chapter 23

In The House of My Lord

Needing a director for their medical/surgical unit, San Joaquin Community Hospital took the risk of hiring someone who had been out of hospital nursing much too long. So, we were soon on our way to Bakersfield, California. Having lived in Bakersfield before (soon after Dick and I had married), this location was not my first choice, but that is where the job was. We settled into a home. Al found work at Pacific Health Education Center as a Bible instructor, and I went to work at the hospital.

Stories had circulated on the unit that I was a tough army nurse. They were relieved to find the rumors were false. I was amazed to observe what had happened to hospitals while I was doing other things. Yes, I had heard about the changes, but experiencing it for myself was something quite different! When I left American nursing, hospitals had been service-oriented institutions. Now, thanks to new government regulations, the bottom line was all-important. Staff was cut to the bare bone. Adding up the time it would take a nurse to do all the duties expected, there obviously was never enough time in any one day to complete the tasks.

After working a few months in their medical/surgical unit, a position as employee health nurse became available, and I requested a change. I had no experience in employee health, but I looked forward to the challenge. This was a new department, so I could organize it as I wished. My boss, Jeff Eller, was very supportive of what I wanted to do. He provided funds to set up computer programming to track employee immunizations and to follow many other things. Another part of my responsibility was to oversee employee on-the-job injuries. Having never worked in this area, I took evening classes from the community college, which explained the rules concerning workers' compensation. With permission, I worked to change the protocol of treating injured employees at our hospital. Within a couple years, I saved the hospital many times over the cost of my salary and equipment.

I soon received an exciting phone call from Evert. Carmen was in labor at the hospital. I made arrangements to fly out the next morning to welcome little Christina home. Carmen had always been fascinated by babies, even when she was not much more than a baby herself. Her pregnancy was a wonderful time for her, and the new baby brightened their home. Too bad Grandma Iris lived so far away! Having a baby changed their lives more than they anticipated, but they adjusted, as parents do. Three years later Trevor was added to the family.

Proud parents. Of course I had to go see the new arrival.

In Bakersfield, we once again formed good friendships with the people at the Hillcrest Church and entered into their activities. The pastor believed their church had need for women elders, and the nominating committee asked me and two other women to serve in that position. One of the ladies refused because she believed this issue could split the church. The second lady and I accepted what the nominating committee asked us to do. The pastor handled it skillfully, and it caused no split in the church, although some continued to oppose the concept.

Al's son, Doug, and his family decided to move to Bakersfield to set up a painting business in Bakersfield. We enjoyed spending good times with them. It took some time to get started, but eventually Doug built himself up a thriving business.

To get out of the heat in the summertime, we headed for Mt. Pinos and to other nearby places of higher elevation. When we had a free weekend, we went to Hart Park and Morro Bay, which I particularly enjoyed because there were so many birds. Occasionally, we drove to Loma Linda to see Rosy, who was now on the faculty of Loma Linda University.

One sad day the phone rang to tell us that Mom had fallen and had a fractured hip. (Hadn't she had enough trouble with her legs?) She was in the hospital in Spencer, Iowa and was scheduled for surgery. We children discussed via phone how we could help her. I agreed to be the first one to go home to care for her when she returned from the hospital. The surgeon gave me a projected date as to when she would be released. On that day I was at the hospital to help with her discharge. However, the nurses told me they didn't think Mom would be going anywhere, as she had experienced a set-back. She had developed pneumonia, and the following day it took her life. How glad I was that I had returned home to be with her.

Once again the family gathered for a funeral. Through all the years, the Ruthven farm in Iowa had remained home to all us children and to our children. As life had moved us here and there across America and around the world, this farm had been the one stable place where we could always return. We were thankful that Mom had died quickly, for she would not have wanted it any other way. To be cared for as an invalid would have been a horror to her, but, of course, her death and the loss of our home base was a painful experience for us. Once again we determined we should meet together for happier occasions. (We have kept that agreement, and we have also kept in touch via email.)

Al retired from Pacific Health and took up his paint brush again. In Kirkland, he had operated a painting business. Now in Bakersfield he worked with Doug for a while, but soon Al had as many jobs as he wished. There was one major problem, though, he could not tolerate heat. In Bakersfield, summers could be very hot, and over the years, Al suffered a number of heat strokes. When I turned 62 years old, he announced that since I now had other options (social security), I could retire, and we should move to a cooler place.

He thought we could live on social security, but I didn't think that was adequate. He reminded me that we would

Death brought sadness, but God provided another joy. Trevor arrived. Christina is being introduced to her new brother.

have enough income from the sale of our house to buy another house wherever we moved. San Joaquin Hospital had matching retirement funding to which I had been contributing. If I chose to take that route, we would have that money. When I reached 65, I would have some denominational retirement income coming; however, it would be somewhat reduced because I had move to San Joaquin rather than continuing with denominational employment. On the other hand, my salary for the past five years had been much higher than I had received either as a missionary or at the GC, so my social security was set at a higher rate. I didn't know all the exact differences, but we took the leap. I turned in my resignation, which would become effective at the end of May, 1996.

Our house sold rather quickly. Some of our things were put into the fifth-wheel we had purchased a couple years before, and some were put in storage. Our new-found freedom beckoned us northward to Alaska for the summer. Al and I had taken an Alaskan trip by water earlier with Dick's sister, Carolyn, and her family, and now we wanted to see it by land. After traveling all the surfaced roads of Alaska that summer, cooler weather let us know that fall was around the corner, and snow was not far behind. So, after enjoying the spectacular scenery and meeting many wonderful people, it was time to head south again, but where should we go?

By then we knew that living in a fifth-wheel for long periods of time did not appeal to us. We also recognized that even though we were retirees, we did not want to live only to entertain ourselves. That did not fit our view of a Christian lifestyle. We were ready to settle somewhere and get involved with another church. A retirement book listed Sequim as high on the list of desirable places to retire.

My mind recalled a time when Carmen was in the fifth grade in Kirkland, Washington. For a class outing, I went camping with her class to Olympic National Park. One of the students in her class was Al Stober's son, Doug! I remembered that the peninsula was a beautiful location situated near both water and mountains, but that it had less rain than Seattle. Yes, we would take a look at Sequim, as well as some other places in Washington and Oregon. Since Sequim was the closest to us, we decided to start there.

It was a Friday afternoon when we arrived and found a place to park. Al went into town to look around and to find the location of the church. On Sabbath, everyone at church was friendly. We were even invited to a picnic after church. We found the people at church, in the stores, and on the streets were friendly, so we decided to go no further. Soon we contacted a realtor and purchased a house.

Sequim felt like home. We enjoyed the mountains, the water, and the rarely hot weather. Yes, it rained at times, and it was grey at times, but even on those days, we delighted in the ever-changing cloud patterns.

An unexpected plus for living in Sequim was an opportunity to visit Ivan's daughter, Heidi, and her family. Heidi was married to a minister in the Washington Conference, and they had two wonderful little boys. An even greater plus was that every now and again, Ivan and Barbara came to see them—and us! This was a rare opportunity we seldom had enjoyed previously because they lived in far-away Missouri.

Eventually, Al and I both served as church elders in the Sequim church. Now, for a number of years, I (with heavy support from Al) have been director of the community services. As of the time we wrote this book, we feel satisfaction at still being useful for the Lord.

Looking back, I stand in awe at how God has led me, but the journey is not finished. It will not be until I see my Jesus face to face. It will not be until I am reunited with Dick and Richie and Rodney. I can hardly wait to see Dick's face when Carmen introduces him to Evert, Christina and Trevor. I want Dick to meet Al and his family; I want to tell Dick what a blessing they have been to Carmen and me. I want to tell the boys about the time when the Communist rebels held a gun in my face and about getting stuck in Nigeria. Oh, I have so many stories to share with Richie and Rodney. I can hardly wait for those good times when I will dwell in the house of my Lord. I know that when Jesus comes, I will be with my loved ones—so many!—Mom and Dad, Stella and my family and friends from around the world. Then there will be no more good-byes. There will be no more separation or crying because it will last forever and forever and forever. Amen and Amen.

Epilogue

Stella: Has four children who all grew up in Alaska and are living productive lives.

MaryEtta: Married Bud Brose and has six children. Worked as a newspaper editor. After being widowed, married Don Hidde and is now retired in South Dakota.

Rosy: Has two boys. Was director of health information systems at a number of hospitals, chair of the department of health information systems at Loma Linda University. Is retired in Texas.

Shirley: Married Herbert Messinger and has four children. Worked as food service director at Blue Mountain Academy and Walla Walla College. Is retired in Washington.

Lyle: Married Arlene Burchett and has four children. Worked as a math teacher, principal of academies, and superintendent of education for the Texas conference. Holds a doctorate in education. Is retired in Texas.

Grace: Married Bob Wells and has two sons. Worked as a security officer at Gates Rubber Co. Is retired in Texas.

Ivan: Married Barbara Stearman and has three children. Worked as a copy machine repairman. Is retired in Georgia.

Jack: Married RoseMarie Beltz and has two sons. Worked as a special education teacher/principal. Is retired in Alaska.

Carolyn: Married Burton Briggs and had two daughters. Worked as a nurse before losing her battle with cancer.

Doug: Married Kim Pease and has a step-daughter and daughter. Developed Diversified Painting.

Carmen: Married Evert McDowell and has two children. Worked as an OB and recovery nurse and is now working in a cardiac clinic.

Dyvonne: Married Craig Keyport and has four children. Works as a medical record transcriber.

We invite you to view the complete
selection of titles we publish at:

www.TEACHServices.com

Scan with your mobile
device to go directly
to our website.

Please write or email us your praises, reactions,
or thoughts about this or any other book we publish at:

P.O. Box 954
Ringgold, GA 30736

info@TEACHServices.com

TEACH Services, Inc., titles may be purchased in bulk for
educational, business, fund-raising, or sales promotional use.
For information, please e-mail:

BulkSales@TEACHServices.com

Finally, if you are interested in seeing
your own book in print, please contact us at

publishing@TEACHServices.com

We would be happy to review your manuscript for free.

www.ingramcontent.com/pod-product-compliance
Lightning Source LLC
Chambersburg PA
CBHW082231180426
43200CB00037B/2820